INSIDE THE
CHRISTMAS STORY

INSIDE THE CHRISTMAS STORY

Reflections for Advent

ANTHONY AND MELANIE BASH

B L O O M S B U R Y

LONDON • NEW DELHI • NEW YORK • SYDNEY

First published in Great Britain 2012

© Anthony and Melanie Bash

The moral right of the authors has been asserted
No part of this book may be used or reproduced in any manner
whatsoever without written permission from the Publisher except in
the case of brief quotations embodied in critical articles or reviews.
Every reasonable effort has been made to trace copyright holders of
material reproduced in this book, but if any have been inadvertently
overlooked the Publishers would be glad to hear from them.

Bloomsbury Publishing Plc
50 Bedford Square
London WC1B 3DP

www.bloomsbury.com

Bloomsbury Publishing, London, Berlin, New York and Sydney
A CIP record for this book is available from the British Library.

ISBN 978 1 4411 2158 5
10 9 8 7 6 5 4 3 2 1

Typeset by Newgen Imaging Systems Pvt Ltd, Chennai, India
Printed in India

*To Morna D. Hooker and
Alison and Stephen Morley in deep gratitude
for their influence in our lives*

CONTENTS

FOREWORD

It was the late Cardinal Hume who once suggested that it was about time that we put Christ back in to Christmas. And that is precisely the aim of Melanie and Anthony Bash in this excellent collection of thoughts and reflections for the season of Advent, itself much in danger of being almost wholly marginalized even by the churches themselves.

From the first day of December until the day after Christmas, the reader is presented with a clear and accessible 'thought for the day' which is deeply rooted in Scripture, and in particular the birth narratives of Matthew and Luke. And whereas it may have been more convenient either to evade or avoid altogether some of the more challenging passages, Melanie and Anthony tackle, for example, the opening genealogy of the Gospel of Matthew and the belief in the virginal birth of Jesus head-on, ensuring a refreshingly lively and vigorous examination of the text, as well as an appropriately relevant interpretation for the day.

As might be expected too in Advent – with the seasonal emphasis on the 'last things' – the authors of *Inside the Christmas Story*, reflecting on and thinking through their own personal vocations and professional 'hands-on' experiences, make the collection truly 'come to life'. They include as well some elements that will disturb and challenge the reader with questions and messages which are in no way either smug, self-satisfied or comfortable. Furthermore, their contributions neither sermonize nor moralize.

In all, here are 26 pieces about Advent which recall the reader to its true purpose, namely an invitation not simply to be carried along with the ways of the world, as if in Advent Christmas had already arrived, but rather to take the trouble to stop and look and listen expectantly and excitedly to the 'word of the Lord' each of the days before Christmas. The result is that when the Day finally arrives, it can be celebrated with even greater joy and thanksgiving – the day on which 'the Word became flesh and dwelt among us' and a day which brings good tidings of great joy for all people.

+David, Lord Hope of Thornes
Archbishop of York (1995–2005)

PREFACE

We would like to thank the Right Reverend and Right Honourable The Lord Hope of Thornes, former Archbishop of York, for reading this book and for his generous words in the Foreword.

To friends who have read the book (in part or in whole) in draft or who have discussed it with us, we would also like to record our thanks. They include (in alphabetical order) J. D. G. ('Jimmy') Dunn, Angus and Sarah Goudie, Peter MacLellan, Walter Moberly, Geoffrey Scarre and Miranda Threlfall-Holmes.

Though the reflections are not co-authored, we have thought about them together and they reflect our joint thinking. We write as committed Christians in the traditions of the developed faith of the Church. Melanie is a practising clinical psychologist working for the NHS. She has written the reflections headed 12, 18, 21, 22 and 23 December. In writing them, she has brought to bear her Christian faith on her clinical experience. Anthony has written the remainder of the book and writes as a Christian minister who has a background teaching the New Testament to University students.

The quotations from the Bible have been translated by Anthony. The translations are intended to capture the spirit, as well as the literal sense, of the original languages.

Anthony and Melanie Bash

Durham, 2012

Before we begin . . .

Before we begin, it might help if we make a few observations.

The observations may seem obvious to you, but their implications are not always straightforward.

First, Christmas is a *Christian* festival to celebrate the birth of Jesus Christ.

However, when Christmas is set in the public arena, Christmas is often a *secular* celebration, reshaped to include all people and to offend none.

Advertisers and marketing executives have made sure that Christmas, that mid-winter festival of spending money, is for everyone, whoever they are, whether they have faith or no faith and whether they belong in a Christian tradition or not.

Secondly, Advent,[1] a period of a little less than a month before Christmas, is not a time principally for making mince pies and

---

[1] Advent is from a Latin word and means 'coming'. The 'coming' that is referred to is the coming of Christ, born as a human being. The first day of Advent is always a Sunday and is the first of the four Sundays immediately before Christmas. Advent is also regarded as a time of preparation for the 'second coming' of Jesus Christ as judge at the end of time. In former times, fasting was practised during Advent. The last day of Advent is Christmas Eve.

icing Christmas cakes, for buying presents, putting up decorations or writing cards (though, of course, many of us rightly do these things).

Rather, Advent is a season of personal and corporate preparation. It is a time for Christians to get ready to celebrate God's wonderful gift of Jesus at the first Christmas. It is a time to reflect on how to celebrate wisely and appropriately.

Thirdly, the materialistic and secular mindset of the twenty-first century increasingly affects how Christians celebrate Christmas. Commercial and social pressures tend to shape what Christians do, rather more than Scripture and the traditions of the Church.

Lastly, each year there seem to be fewer and fewer connections between the Christian religious base of what Christmas is about and what (and who) people at large are celebrating. In a nutshell, Jesus has got more and more forgotten about at Christmas.

If these observations strike a chord with you, this book is for you!

So please read on if you want to *reflect on the first Christmas* without its sentimental and commercial trappings.

Read on if you want to move from the sanitized, mythical Jesus of popular culture (like Father Christmas or the tooth fairy) to worship the deeply disconcerting God whose presence and activities run through the Christmas story.

Read on if you want to rediscover that the Christmas story takes us to the heart of Christian discipleship.

In short, we hope we will get *inside the Christmas story*, not only to discover its wonder and joys but also to acknowledge its turmoil and heartaches. We hope too that the Christmas story will get *inside us*. The result, most likely, is that our faith will deepen and our lives will change.

This book consists of a series of reflections, mainly on the first two chapters of each of the Gospels of Matthew and Luke. These chapters – only 180 verses in total – comprise most of the material we have in the New Testament on the birth of Jesus and the surrounding events.

The reflections in this book can be read during Advent and for two days beyond, at the rate of one each day of December until (and including) 26 December. This is how we have written them to be read. (The reason for going two days beyond the end of Advent will become obvious when you read the reflections headed 25 and 26 December.)

However, the reflections may be read at *any* time of the year and in *any* way you wish. Taken that way, this book explores the implications of the birth of Jesus and what people now call 'the incarnation' in a series of 'bite-sized' reflections.

In whichever way you read the book, we have tried to recover and to re-establish the Christian roots of Christmas. We hope the result will be that you understand the first Christmas in a new way – and in a way that is relevant to life today. We also hope that you will encounter the loving, disturbing, turbulent, dazzling God whose imprint is on every part of the Christmas story.

The reflections are sometimes not comfortable to read. They have not been comfortable to write. Even so, they have helped us to understand more of what it means that 'God was in Christ reconciling the world to himself . . . and entrusting to us the message of salvation' (2 Corinthians 5.19).

Christmas . . . and Jesus

What then shall I do with Jesus?

MATTHEW 27.22

Sometimes on television, in the weeks before Christmas, children are interviewed and asked to say what Christmas means to them.

It is easy to smile at what they say.

Sometimes, they talk about the presents they receive, the food they eat and the television programmes they watch. The more reflective may also refer to eccentric relatives who visit, or aunts whose clothes smell strange, or grandparents who want to listen to the Queen's speech.

Only rarely will they speak about Jesus.

It is not that they are embarrassed to speak about Jesus. It is that, so far as they know, Jesus is irrelevant for Christmas.

These children are no different from many adults who also think Christmas to be more-or-less religion-free, because for them, too, there is no obvious link between Jesus and Christmas.

In some contexts, it is now unacceptable even to refer to an overtly 'Christian' aspect to Christmas. This is because some insist, for the sake of inclusivity, that the celebration of Christmas in a public setting should be denuded of its Christian origin. So Christmas cards will say 'Season's Greetings' (to avoid a reference to the Christian origin of the festival) and public decorations will be faith-neutral (to avoid supposed offence to those who are not Christians). Some groups even celebrate Christmas at the same time as and without distinguishing it from other winter events.[1] For them, Christmas is just one of a variety of mid-winter diversions.

Christmas is becoming like any other secular celebration, such as Thanksgiving in the United States or Guy Fawkes Night in Britain, except that at Christmas, we spend more money and there is a longer build-up. Many think of Christmas to be no more than the name for a break from work in the middle of the winter, the season of mince pies, presents, turkeys, cards and decorated trees.

---

[1]Birmingham City Council in England celebrates 'Winterval' (formed from the words 'winter' and 'festival'). This new festival combines neo-pagan celebrations (such as the winter solstice), the Jewish festival of Hanukkah, the Muslim festivals of Ramadan (occasionally, according to when the festival falls) and Eid, the Hindu festival of Diwali and the secular New Year's Day holiday.

Of course, some elements of the Christian origins of Christmas remain, though detached from their context and significance. For example, everyone (well, almost everyone) loves a newborn baby. There is something very appealing (and safe) about remembering that Jesus came as a baby in a stable, with shepherds and three wise men, in mid-winter. Many schools put on nativity plays and shops still play carols as background music.

Even so, ask most people what Christmas is about, and I suspect they would say, 'Presents, families, time off work and food'. Sadly, some may want to add, 'Stress and debt'. Increasingly few would say that Christmas is to celebrate the birth of Jesus.

Confusion and ignorance about Jesus are not new.

For example, when Pontius Pilate was questioning Jesus shortly before he ordered Jesus' execution, Pilate was troubled because he could not match what Jesus' accusers were saying with what his own senses were telling him.

It was evident to Pilate that Jesus was not a political insurrectionist and he did not present a threat to Roman power. It was also clear to Pilate that the threat Jesus presented was to the interests of the Jewish leaders and to the religious status quo in which those leaders had such a large stake.

Pilate was weak. Under pressure from the Jews, Pilate agreed to release a notorious terrorist called Barabbas and to have Jesus executed. This was against Pilate's own better judgement. It was despite his wife's unease about what was happening to Jesus. It was also despite the fact that Barabbas represented far more of a political, military and social threat than Jesus did.

The question Pilate did not want to face with courage was this: Which Jesus was before him? Was it the Jesus his senses told him was present, someone inconvenient to the Romans (because he had upset the Jews), but not a threat? Or was it the Jesus the Jews insisted that he was, a threat to public order and safety, and a threat to Roman rule?

When the Jewish leaders asked Pilate to release Barabbas, Pilate said, 'So then, what do you want me to do with Jesus?'[2] The implication of his question is that, surely, the Jewish leaders did not wish Pilate to execute someone he believed to be an innocent man. The tragic reply was 'Crucify him'.

We sometimes hear sermons about Jesus and Barabbas. The Romans executed Jesus and spared Barabbas. The point is often made that Jesus did not deserve to die (as he had committed no crime) but Barabbas did, because he had committed capital crimes. With this in mind, preachers sometimes make a link between Jesus taking the place of Barabbas and the atoning death of Jesus for us.

I do not want to focus on that link.

---

[2]Matthew 27.22.

Rather, what I want to explore is another type of substitution. It is this: Which Jesus are *we* celebrating and remembering at Christmas? Is it the Jesus of popular imagination at Christmas or is it the Jesus of the Gospels in his historical and cultural setting? Is the Jesus we are celebrating the Jesus who has been more shaped by the secular world around us than disclosed in Holy Scripture?

We can smile at the Jesus in a Christmas story that is safe, sentimental and sugary. The media have reshaped this Jesus to be tame and domesticated so as not to ruffle us.

In contrast, the real Jesus of the Christmas story can speak to us, challenge us and even unsettle us. So too can God his father, who is so evidently behind the events of the story. More than that: the Christmas story itself, with its accounts of political intrigue, unexpected pregnancies, displaced people, heartache and a massacre of children, addresses issues of life that are timeless and deeply troubling. Where is God in these events, and how can we blend them into a faith that does not give up on a God of love and mercy?

As we engage with Christmas without the sentimental and commercial trappings of the season, we free ourselves to discover more about the person whose birth Christians celebrate. We are also likely to discover more of what it means to be a disciple. The Christmas story, properly understood, can draw us into deeper faith and worship. It can also sometimes leave us challenged, awed and even occasionally frightened.

I admit that I am deeply frustrated throughout the season of Advent (more popularly known as the 'run-up' to Christmas) because so much seems to get in the way of finding time to explore the Christmas story as it is meant to be read and understood. The noise, the excitement and the pressure to get everything ready on time bother me.

It does not have to be like this. We can choose to be different and to make time to re-engage with Advent and Christmas. We can resolve to ignore, as best we can, the mythical Jesus of popular culture who has been reconstructed to make us feel comfortable and at ease. Instead, we can make time and interior space to rediscover the Jesus of the New Testament, who disturbs, unsettles and brings change.

Which Jesus will be your focus?

I hope it will be the Jesus whom we discover in the New Testament. This Jesus has changed human history. This Jesus has pointed us to the way to God. This Jesus is the subject of this book.

DECEMBER 2

Christmas . . . and the rest of life

For everything, there is a season. For every matter under heaven, there is a right time.

ECCLESIASTES 3.1

Life's problems and issues do not go away at Christmas, and if we think they do, we are fooling ourselves.

The media, the shops and the advertisers would have us believe that we can have the 'perfect' Christmas.

They seem to suggest that if we buy the right decorations, put out the best tableware, give and receive the right presents, buy, cook and eat the right food, then the issues we face on a day-to-day basis will evaporate.

Just whom are they deceiving?

Will the right decorations, tableware, presents and food change a selfish spouse for the better? Will they make a chronic disease go away? Will they mend a broken relationship or bring back a loved one who has died?

Of course not, and we know that . . . and yet we hope *this* Christmas will be different.

I once heard an illustration that has stuck in my mind as being wise and true.

It concerns a couple – let us call them Jim and Fiona – who had an acrimonious divorce.

When Jim and Fiona split up, Jim moved out of the home that he and Fiona had lived in for many years. Just before he went, Jim put some frozen prawns inside the hollow of a large, brass curtain rail in the lounge.

As the weeks went by, Fiona could not understand where the smell in the lounge was coming from. The smell got worse and worse. It became so bad that she decided that she would have to sell the house and buy another.

You can probably guess what happened next.

When Fiona sold the house, she took the curtain rail with her. Soon, the smell in her new house was just as bad as the smell in the old house.

In our family, we have a saying that, like Fiona, 'We take our prawns with us.'

By this, we mean that the issues we face on a day-to-day basis often do not go away just because it is, for example, someone's birthday, or that we have gone out for a meal, or that we are on holiday. We are still the same people, with the same needs and weaknesses. A change of scene or a new activity or a visitor does not mean we are different people without the weaknesses, foibles and idiosyncrasies we had before. We still have our prawns because they are still with us.

'Taking our prawns with us' also means that at Christmas, many of the issues we face on a day-to-day basis remain.

We know this but sometimes we do not admit or face up to it.

We know that difficult relatives do not become easy for that one day of the year. We know that unhappy marriages frequently become even unhappier at Christmas because of the weight of expectation. We know that debts remain debts. We know that unemployed family members remain unemployed. We know that illness remains illness.

If you are following what I have been saying, you may realize at this point what has gone wrong with the modern idea of Christmas.

Christmas is not necessarily about a different sort of day (though it may be). Neither is Christmas always about you or me enjoying the day (though I hope we will). Nor is it about what we receive or what we give (though many of us enjoy both of these). It is not about families, children, holidays or . . . I leave it to you to add to the list, as you wish.

Christmas is about *celebrating* the fact that God, through Jesus, now points humanity to faith, to life, to hope and to peace.

It is about an astonishing, supernatural event that was heralded by signs in the sky, angels appearing, a virginal conception and prophecies being fulfilled. It is about the birth of a child in a backwater of the Roman Empire. It is about a child whose adult life, teaching and example have changed the course of history.

We can celebrate this on *any* day of the year, and in *any* way we choose that is appropriate.[1] We can celebrate if we are ill, or bereaved, or unemployed, or in debt, or worried . . . or happy, fulfilled and contented. We can celebrate the wonder of what God has done whichever issues, good or bad, we may face in life. Whoever we are, we can *each* celebrate Christmas.

In former days, with what I think was great wisdom, many of the churches in the Western world instituted a period of self-reflection and preparation before Christmas. It is called 'Advent', as I have already explained on p. 1. It is a season of penitence and self-denial, though one would not guess this from much of what we see today, even in churches. The aim of the season is to make us ready to celebrate Christmas as we ought.

For those whose churches observe such customs, 'purple' is usually the liturgical colour for Advent.[2] Purple is also usually

---

[1] The date of Christmas is arbitrary, as we do not know the date when Jesus was born.

[2] In some Christian traditions, an exception is made on the third Sunday of Advent. On that Sunday, rose-coloured (not purple) vestments may be worn.

the colour for 'Lent', another of the seasons of penitence and preparation in the calendar of the Church.

Both seasons, Advent and Lent, are opportunities the Church gives to help people to be ready to celebrate two great events in the Christian year: the birth of Jesus (after Advent) and the resurrection of Jesus (after Lent). They both involve a period of preparation before an important celebration.

There is great wisdom in taking time to prepare to celebrate. We need to be ready, and to feel ready, as many people who have been the 'victims' of surprise parties will know.

I still recall a friend who threw a surprise thirtieth birthday party for his wife in their home. I was one of the guests. We were asked to hide in a room of our friend's house. We heard his wife return home from a shopping trip and, in order to ensure his wife would be ready for the party, we heard her husband suggest she go and change, pretending they were to go out for a meal. 'No', she said. 'I would like a hot bath and an early night. And anyway, I don't want to go out. My hair looks awful, and I have nothing to wear.' In vain, he tried to persuade her to change her mind so that she would be ready for the surprise party. We heard the whole conversation from our hiding place. In the end, he had to tell her what was going on. (I would not have liked to hear what this couple said to one another after the party.)

We said in the previous reflection that this book is for those who want to rediscover Jesus for Christmas.

There is another purpose to this book. It is to help us to prepare (and so be ready) for Christmas and for all Christmas can mean in whichever circumstances we may find ourselves. Perhaps we are doing this during Advent. If so, we are grounding our preparations on a seasonal tradition of the Church. We can also prepare to celebrate the birth of Jesus at *any* time of the year; we certainly do not have to wait for or confine ourselves to the time traditionally set by the Church for this.

In helping us to prepare for Christmas, we are seeking to put back the purple into Advent and, some might add, to put a little bit of Lent into Advent.

Before you read on, may I suggest you make a promise to yourself that this year you will *prepare* to celebrate the birth of Jesus?

Of course, as you are reading this book, I hope it will help you to prepare. You may also have to learn to say 'no' to some of the self-imposed yokes of the modern Christmas season: exactly the right presents, precisely the right food, always a new recipe for a dessert, and so on. Perhaps we should all also seek to be less busy and preoccupied with the demands of the season. If we do, we may find we have more time for prayer, for reading and for family and friends.

Now we begin in detail our reflections on the birth of Jesus by exploring the richness, the vigour and the challenges of the Christmas story.

Christmas . . . and science

The word became flesh and dwelt among us.
JOHN 1.14

A distinguished scientist once wrote to me, 'I cannot see why/ how anyone educated and rational can believe in such a thing as a God'.

In this reflection, I would like to explore the significance of the Christmas story for responding to what the scientist wrote. I begin with a story about a goldfish (a scientifically and philo-sophically minded goldfish) that was in a goldfish bowl, trying to understand its watery world.

The goldfish knows that there are stones, rocks and plants in its bowl. It is vaguely aware of blurred objects to which it can-not swim and which seem a long way away. (These are objects in the room outside the goldfish bowl.) The fish also knows that a moving figure comes into view once a day, to drop food into the bowl.

If the fish could talk and if you were to ask the fish about its world, what would the fish say?

I suspect that the answer is that the fish would not, and could not, say very much. The fish cannot be objective because it cannot be external to its world. It can only describe its world as it experiences it, rather than have (from our perspective) what would be full knowledge of it. At best, the goldfish can explore, observe and verify its goldfish bowl and what is in it, but this can be only from within it.

Even when the goldfish explores its goldfish bowl, it cannot find out much. For example, it cannot analyse what water consists of, where the water comes from or why the water does not fall out of the goldfish bowl. Neither can it say who or what put the bowl where it is.

When it comes to what is outside the goldfish bowl, the fish cannot be certain about the objects and moving figures that it sees from time to time. All it can do is to say to itself that it is aware of things outside the goldfish bowl and that it cannot verify these things. It may also wonder whether anything exists beyond the visible space (the room) in which the bowl stands.

The fish will also have a choice to make about what questions it can legitimately ask. There are at least four overlapping questions that it may ask. They are as follows:

- Will it say that it can only enquire about what it can verify?

- Will it live with the hope that one day it will have answers to its questions about what is in the bowl and why it is there? (We know that that hope is misplaced, but the goldfish does not.)

- Will it be prepared to recognize that there *are* things or beings external to the goldfish bowl, even though it can observe only some of them and wonder about others?

- Will it dismiss what is 'outside' the bowl because what is outside cannot be verified?

Whichever questions the fish may choose to answer, from our point of view it would still be very limited in what it could know or understand.

The situation of human beings is similar. There is much that we can explore, describe, verify and classify. However, we live with many unanswered questions. We also have questions that are *impossible* for us to answer because we are part of the world that we are seeking to describe. We will also have to decide whether what we cannot verify is the legitimate subject of enquiry and even belief.

If the goldfish were to have an enlarged understanding, someone or something from outside the goldfish bowl would have to tell it what it cannot know by its own efforts. It would also have to believe that such a person or thing is indeed speaking to it. (If the fish believed that such a person or thing could *not* do that, it would disregard what the person or thing appears to say, and the fish would be no wiser.) Such a person or thing would have to tell the goldfish what water consists of, where water comes from or why the water does not fall out of the goldfish bowl. It would also have to tell the fish who or what put the bowl where it is and what exists outside the goldfish bowl. The fish, no matter how clever, would not be able to work out these things for itself, though it may be able to make the odd good guess.

You will, of course, see how what I have been telling you about our scientifically and philosophically minded goldfish relates to the Christmas story.

Christmas marks the point when someone was born into the world who could tell us, in a way and in a depth that no other human being before or since has been able to do, things about God we could not know by our own endeavours. This person supremely revealed the God of Judaism, who is also the God in whom Christians believe. He did this by who he was and by what he did and taught. Through him, what could otherwise only be guessed was disclosed.

The person who came did more than reveal the God of Judaism (as if that were not enough!): during his brief adult life, he also invited people freely to respond to the God of love whom he disclosed and whom he modelled. He said they should love God with all their being.[1]

We sometimes call what happened on the first Christmas day 'the incarnation'. That means, in the developed understanding of Christianity, that God became a human being and, by becoming a human being, continued a process of self-disclosure that had been going on for thousands of years.

However, some will want to say that it is irrational and unscientific to believe in this disclosure because we cannot scientifically verify (that is, prove beyond any shadow of doubt) what has now been disclosed. Others will want to go further and say that it is not meaningful even to *acknowledge* such disclosure because it is impossible for its accuracy to be scientifically proven. In other words, such people are saying that if we cannot demonstrate something scientifically, it is not meaningful even to admit that it may exist. (I think this underlies what the scientist who wrote to me meant.)

---

[1]See Matthew 22.34–40, for example.

I suspect that it is *not* possible to demonstrate beyond any shadow of doubt that God exists. Similarly, we *cannot* demonstrate beyond a shadow of doubt that the content of divine disclosure is true.

In my view, this does not mean that it is foolish or irrational to believe in God or in the content of divine disclosure. True, there is not the same degree of evidence about these matters as one might expect from scientific endeavour; nevertheless, there is evidence.

Many people – many *sane* people – speak of knowing that there are spiritual realities that they cannot prove but which they have experienced. They speak in terms of the self-disclosure of the God who is 'out there' who touches their lives and changes the way they view the world. Among these people are some of the most subtle and profound thinkers the world has known.

For Christians, an important reason why it makes sense to believe in God is that on the first Easter Sunday there was an empty tomb and that God raised Jesus from the dead.

We all know that we will die. Death is even more certain than taxes![2] Christians say that by raising Jesus from the dead, God demonstrated more cogently than in any way before that

---

[2]This phrase is adapted from what Benjamin Franklin (1706–90) wrote to Jean-Baptiste Leroy in 1789: 'In this world nothing can be said to be certain, except death and taxes.'

there is a God and that the limitations we human beings face (such as death) do not constrict God. Many regard the reversal of death through a resurrection as a persuasive reason for believing that there is a God.

Other people have been persuaded to believe in God because, after the first Easter Sunday, frightened, ineffective and relatively uneducated men and women were transformed through their experience of the resurrection. Some willingly faced martyrdom. From these early followers in a backwater of the Roman Empire, a worldwide and (despite what the press say) still vibrant movement developed. Modern members of that movement claim a share in the same (apparently perverse and unscientific) transforming experience of those first-century people.

To conclude from the lack of the sort of evidence and testing that one would use for scientific enquiry that it is irrational to believe in God is, I believe, misguided. This is, I believe, to make what philosophers call 'a mistake of category', for it is a mistake to insist on the same mode of testing that one expects of the material and tangible world of reality to establish claims about an altogether different world of reality. To put it more colloquially, this is 'mixing apples and pears'.

One can go further and say that there is no reason why all things should be scientifically provable. (Anyway, as neither scientists nor philosophers can prove that there is something rather than nothing yet assume that there *is* something, they do not always follow their chosen method of investigation and proof.) It is important to remain open to things that may not be capable of scientific proof. This is what it means to be a mature human being: open-minded, curious and capable of learning and changing.

To return to our main theme, without Christmas, we would be less confident that there is a God. Because of Christmas, the God who is 'out there' has now disclosed himself, more fully than ever before, within the constraints of our material existence. Without Easter, the claims about the disclosure would also be less solid.

Of course, we need more than mere intellectual assent that God has disclosed himself at the first Christmas. The one whom he sent invites all people to trust God, to love him and to put into practice what he asks of men and women. Much of the rest of this book explores what it means to do these things.

It is neither irrational nor foolish nor perverse to believe in God. With both faith *and* intellectual rigour, Christians can celebrate the fact that God has spoken to human beings through Jesus and that God is calling people to believe in him. We can sing with heartfelt gratitude the (originally Latin) carol, 'O come, all ye faithful' and celebrate the fact that the 'Word of the Father' has indeed appeared in flesh.

Christmas . . . and the Gospels of Matthew and Luke

After making a careful investigation . . . I decided to write an ordered account . . . so that you may know the truth.

LUKE 1.3, 4

The accounts of the birth of Jesus do not begin with the words, 'Once upon a time . . .', as one might expect if we were reading a story or myth. Neither do the accounts end, 'And they all lived happily ever after.'

None of us knows when Cinderella was born, or where she lived; and none of us knows where Jack's beanstalk grew. (If we did, we might go and look to see if we too could find a golden egg.) Inveterate fans of the *Star Wars* series of films (like me) will know that the events portrayed in the first of the films to be made happened 'a long time ago, in a galaxy far, far away', but (as far as I know) we are not told which galaxy or when.[1]

In contrast, we are given the accounts of Jesus' birth as rooted in fact, historically verifiable and shaped by the uncertainties of social and political forces. They are not in a form that one would expect of fable or myth.

Matthew's account begins with a genealogy based (probably) on Temple genealogical records.[2] He records Jesus as a member of Joseph and Mary's family, though he is careful *not* to say that 'Joseph is the father of Jesus.'[3] (We think more about the implications of this in our next reflection.) In the genealogy, Matthew traces Joseph's lineage back to King David and then to Abraham, and so sets Jesus in an historical context, and in a context that was verifiable from records.

Matthew also sets his account of the birth of Jesus in the period of the latter years of the reign of Herod the Great (who ruled from 37–4 BC). Herod's cunning and brutality that Matthew writes about[4] are well documented elsewhere (particularly in the writings of the Jewish historian, Josephus), although outside the Bible there is no reference to the

---

[1]From Episode IV, *A New Hope* (1977).
[2]Matthew 1.1–16.
[3]He is also careful to be consistent with his later statement that Mary and Joseph did not have sexual relations until after Jesus was born (Matthew 1.25).
[4]Matthew 2.1–18.

slaughter in Bethlehem of newborn Jewish boys that Matthew describes.[5]

In his Gospel, Luke writes for someone called 'Theophilus', who might have been a real person, though it is possible that he is an imagined reader, as the name 'Theophilus' means, literally, 'friend of God'. Luke says that his intention is to write 'an ordered account' of what eyewitnesses had seen and heard.[6] He writes that he has investigated his sources carefully because he wanted Theophilus to 'know the truth' about what he had already been, in part, informed. Luke is writing primarily biography about Jesus and the form of his introduction in Luke 1 conforms to the style of biographical prefaces used at the time.

In addition, Luke is careful to set the events of Jesus' birth in their historical context. He refers to an imperial edict from Emperor Caesar Augustus requiring the subject-peoples of the Roman Empire to take part in a census.[7] The census Luke refers to is most likely to be one of a series that took place in different regions of the Empire as part of a co-ordinated policy that Augustus instigated to ensure accurate records for levying taxes.[8] Luke sets the census that took place in Judea in the period 'while Quirinius was governor of Syria'.[9]

---

[5] Matthew 2.16–18.
[6] Luke 1.1–4.
[7] Luke 2.1.
[8] See the reflection headed 14 December.
[9] Luke 2.2.

This last point has caused some difficulties for modern historians because, so far as we know from other records, Quirinius was governor in the period beginning in AD 6/7, about ten years after Herod the Great had died.

Based on what we currently know about Quirinius' governorship, Luke's dating of Jesus' birth creates an apparent conflict with Matthew's dating. Was Jesus' birth, as Matthew says, towards the end of the reign of Herod the Great in about 4 BC?[10] Or was it, as Luke appears to say, not earlier than AD 6/7, during the only period of Quirinius' governorship about which we know? Much academic ink has been spilt on this question, and if you want to know more, I suggest you read a commentary on this point.

Whether Luke made a slip or not, what remains important is that Luke was seeking to write an historical account. Even if he got some of his facts wrong (and historians do make errors from time to time), Luke was seeking, like Matthew, to write fact and not fiction, fable or fantasy.

I suspect that both Luke and Matthew knew that cynics were raising eyebrows about the historical accuracy of a virginal conception and about some of the miraculous happenings at the time of the birth of Jesus. They are therefore each careful

---

[10]Jesus was not born in AD 0 or 1, or 0 BC. The suggestion that Jesus may have been born in 4 BC is not a typographical mistake on my part!

to leave their readers in no doubt that they were writing about events that they believed had happened in history (and not in someone's imagination) and that, as best they could, they had carefully scrutinized and evaluated the evidence.

Matthew and Luke were not only writing biography and history. They were also writing theology. By this, I mean that they deliberately selected and shaped the material they wrote to leave their readers and hearers in no doubt about what they thought the material *meant*. The intention of Matthew and Luke was to guide those who read or heard their Gospels to what Matthew and Luke believed was a right interpretation of the facts.

Matthew and Luke, it seems to me, shared two principal *theological* intentions. The first was to show that God was at work through human events that to some onlookers appeared apparently unconnected with anything God might be doing. The second is that the circumstances surrounding the birth of Jesus point to the fact that Jesus was Israel's long-awaited saviour. (They did also have other intentions, as other parts of this book show.)

Does it surprise or trouble you that Luke and Matthew intentionally wrote an interpretative overview of the events they describe?[11] I hope not. All writers have intentions like theirs, for the presentation of 'bald' facts without an analysis of what the

---

[11]John did the same: see John 20.31.

facts may mean is of little value except to someone who wants 'raw data'.

When we read a text, we should let it speak to us as the writer intended the readers to receive it. We should read the Gospels in the way that they were intended to be received, as historical, biographical and theological accounts of the life of Jesus. We are not the masters of the text to insist how to read or interpret it. Rather, we should enter into the text as learners and listeners of what the writers intended.

As we reflect on the birth accounts of Jesus, there are, I suggest in summary, three important things to bear in mind.

First, the accounts are set in a political, social and geographical context. The Gospel writers intend the readers to see and interpret them as historically verifiable.

Secondly, the purpose of the writers is not to write what we would today call 'myth' or 'fiction'. They intended to write historical fact that they had investigated and carefully evaluated for accuracy.

Thirdly, the accounts offer a theological reflection about the historical events that they refer to and, like all serious historical writing, offer an interpretation of those events.

To read the birth accounts as history, biography and theology may require a change of interpretative mindset for some who read this book. This does not mean that we may not also read the accounts devotionally, to nurture and develop faith. We should read them in *all* these ways to worship God 'in spirit and in truth' (John 4.23).

Now that we have identified what Matthew and Luke were intending to write and how they went about it, we are left with an invitation, perhaps even a challenge. The invitation is that we should believe and trust that Matthew and Luke are honest, careful people, who wrote to nurture faith and to draw people to God.

DECEMBER 5

Christmas . . . and a family tree

*Here follows a record of the family line of Jesus, the Messiah,
who is a descendant of David and a descendant of Abraham.*
MATTHEW 1.1

Most of us skip or, at best, read quickly the genealogical passages in the Old Testament and in the New Testament. (These passages list the succession of family generations and often follow the formula, 'A was the father of B, and B was the father of C . . ', and so on.) The genealogies often do not make riveting reading, and I have only once heard a sermon based on one of the genealogies.

This reflection is on the genealogy at the start of the Gospel of Matthew.

Please, do not skip the reflection because you think it may be boring. (At least wait until you have read it all, before deciding whether it is boring!)

The genealogy discloses some important elements of the way God can work in and with people. I suggest that there are at least three such elements.

First, the opening words of the Gospel of Matthew disclose why Matthew included the genealogy. He says the genealogical record shows that Jesus was a descendant of both King David and of Abraham.

To demonstrate who Jesus' forebears were from a genealogical record was important because certain genetic preconditions had to be fulfilled if someone were to be the Messiah, that is, the long-awaited Saviour of Israel, promised in Scripture and foretold by the prophets.[1] These preconditions were, first, that the Messiah was to be a lineal descendant of Abraham, and so Jewish; and, secondly, that the Messiah was to be a lineal descendant of King David, to whom it had been promised that one of his descendants would be a king forever.[2] Without these two things, Abrahamic and Davidic ancestry, a claim to be the Messiah would fail, no matter what other virtues or attributes a claimant might have.

The genealogies are included to show that Jesus did have both Abrahamic and Davidic ancestry. He *could*, therefore, be

---

[1]'Messiah' means 'anointed one'. In this context, it refers to God's choosing and anointing for the task of redeeming God's people.
[2]See, for example, Genesis 17.1–22 and 2 Samuel 7.12–16. See also Deuteronomy 18.15 19, which people in the time of Jesus understood to be a reference to a messianic descendant of Abraham.

the long-awaited Messiah. Much of the rest of the Gospel shows, additionally, that Jesus *was* the Messiah.

However, a sharp-eyed reader of the genealogy may notice that the genealogy traces Jesus' ancestry through Joseph, not Mary. A sharp-minded reader may then wonder what relevance the genealogy could have to Jesus' ancestry, since Matthew clearly believes that Joseph was not the biological father of Jesus.

By referring to Joseph in this way, Matthew obviously cannot be pointing to the overriding importance of physical descent. Rather, he is pointing to Jesus' legal entitlement to be regarded as Joseph's son. This entitlement arose because Joseph had accepted the role of Jesus' father and acknowledged Jesus to be his son. Jesus thereby acquired, by legal attribution, the rights, responsibilities and privileges of a lineal descendant, but they were not Jesus' by birth.

This has implications for Christians. People become part of the people of God through faith in Christ, and the writers of the New Testament use a variety of metaphors to explain how that happens. One of them is to say that they are 'adopted' as children into God's family[3] and through that adoption, they become children of God and heirs with Christ.

So here, we have two parallel ideas. First, that Jesus became an heir of the Abrahamic and Davidic promises because he was

---

[3]Galatians 4.5.

'adopted' by Joseph. Secondly, that people become heirs with Christ through adoption by faith into God's family. In both cases, it is not genetic descent or birth that counts. It is inclusion by adoption, not as a right, but as a gift of grace.

It was, therefore, no good to say, as some Jews did to John the Baptist, that they had no need for salvation because they 'had Abraham as an ancestor'.[4] Having a particular ancestry did not confer grace or salvation. It is equally valueless for those of us who come from Christian families to think that our genetic descent (that is, being children of Christian parents or that we live in 'a Christian country') will make us Christians or give us faith: we each need personally to respond to the love and grace of God. Inclusion in God's family and sharing in the privileges of being fellow-heirs with Christ come not by inheritance but *only* by faith as a gift of God.

That Jesus shared in an adoption as we do is perhaps another example of what the writer to the Hebrews means when he says that Jesus is like us in every respect.[5] Both Jesus *and* his children know what it means to be adopted and to share the privileges and blessings that come from being adopted.

I said earlier that Matthew's genealogical record discloses some important elements of the way God can work in and with

---

[4] Matthew 3.9.
[5] Hebrews 2.17.

people. We have looked at the first such element. The second element is to show that Jesus' coming was not an accident of history. His coming had been planned, and that planned coming was by a genealogical route that God had set out in advance.[6]

Lastly, the genealogical record also discloses that God chose all sorts of people to be the forebears of Jesus. We could call them 'sinners' or 'saints'; some were both but at different times. In particular, God took people who did things that they should never have done and, in ways we do not understand, integrated what they did into his wider purposes. Out of bad, God made good and brought about what he intended.

Some examples illustrate this point.

First, Jesus is a descendant of Solomon, one of Israel's greatest kings. Solomon's mother was Bathsheba, former wife of Uriah the Hittite. David committed adultery with Bathsheba and then deliberately engineered Uriah's death in war so that David would be free to marry Bathsheba. Despite David's sin, God brought about the birth of Solomon as an indirect result of it.

Other examples are Israelite kings who were forebears of Jesus. Some were corrupt, depraved and godless. We are not given a 'rose-tinted' view of whom Jesus was descended from.

---

[6]This is not the only way that Matthew uses in the Gospel to show that the events of Jesus' life are not accidents of history. In the remainder of his account of the birth of Jesus, for example, he repeatedly says that what took place was in fulfilment of ancient prophecy, as we shall see in the reflection headed 7 December.

One was a king named Manasseh. Manasseh was among the worst of all the kings,[7] though the Old Testament does also say that Manasseh repented towards the end of his life.[8]

We also have two examples of *Gentiles* (that is, non-Jews) who were forebears of Jesus. The first is Rahab, who was a prostitute from Jericho. The second is Ruth, from Moab.[9] The Jewish law was clear that Jews should marry only Jews, and that there were to be no 'mixed marriages'. Even so, Jesus was descended from at least two Gentiles.

So is Matthew's genealogy dull? I think not for several reasons.

First, the genealogy demonstrates that by birth Jesus *could* be the Messiah, not that he was. His life, death and resurrection (as the rest of the Gospel of Matthew shows) demonstrate that he *was* the Messiah.

We also learn that birth does not confer (or preclude) spiritual privileges or the right to inherit God's grace. These privileges or rights come as gifts from God. They are available to all people, not just to a few. With God, our origins count neither for us nor against us. (This latter point is particularly important for people whose parents may not have helped to lay a foundation of faith in their lives. It gives us all hope, because God

---

[7] 2 Kings 21 and 2 Chronicles 33.1–9.
[8] 2 Chronicles 33.12–13.
[9] Matthew 1.5.

comes to us as we are, not where our parents should perhaps have helped us to be.)

Next, we see that Jesus' coming was not an accident of history but an event purposed by God. God intended that the Messiah should come from certain forebears, and Matthew shows that when the Messiah did come, his lineage was as God had said.

Finally, human sin does not necessarily stop God from working. Neither does it prevent God's purposes from being fulfilled. We are never beyond usefulness in God's hands. Jesus' forebears were 'saints' and also 'sinners', and God used both.

Perhaps you do not feel you are significant in the purposes and plans of God, or perhaps you feel you are *very* significant in those plans and purposes.

The truth is that we may never know the outcome of historical processes that God shapes and directs, and we may never know our part in those processes. The longer-term significance of our lives is in God's hands, and in God's hands alone. At best, we walk by faith, not knowing the outcome of that walk, confident that thereby we please God.[10] The lesson from the genealogies is that God can use every one of us, even if our lives and faith seem insignificant or are far from what we believe they should be.

---

[10]Hebrews 11.6.

DECEMBER 6

Christmas . . . and Jesus' parents

The angel said to Mary, 'Mary, do not be afraid, for you are experiencing God's favour.'

LUKE 1.30

Matthew and Mark have very different approaches when it comes to the role and place of Mary in their accounts of the birth of Jesus.

Matthew is primarily interested in Joseph's role, not Mary's role. Mary features almost only in the background. She has little more than a minor place in the focus of the narrative.

Matthew tells of the virginal conception from Joseph's viewpoint. He recounts Joseph's dismay at discovering his fiancée is pregnant, and says nothing about Mary's reactions or responses. He records Joseph's encounter with an angel, and not Mary's (which we know about from the Gospel of Luke).[1]

When the Magi come, Jesus is 'with Mary his mother'.[2] Mary's role here is that of a nurturing mother. Matthew does not indicate anything else about Mary, such as her faith or her obedience to God, for example. When an angel appears a second time, the angel appears again only to Joseph, and not to Mary.[3] As a result, Joseph takes both Jesus *and* Mary (written in that order and referring to Mary not by name but as the child's 'mother') first to Egypt and then back to Palestine.[4] (In these passages, Matthew treats Mary as being dependent and passive, reflecting the way women were expected to be in first-century Palestine.) When it comes to the move to Nazareth, Mary is not even mentioned.[5]

When we turn to the Gospel of Luke, Luke portrays Mary's place and role differently. The one with the 'walk-on part' is Joseph, not Mary. Luke refers to Joseph by name in only 3 of the 120 verses that comprise the account of Jesus' birth;[6] on one other occasion, he calls him the 'father' of Jesus.[7]

In the Gospel of Luke, Mary is not an appendage of Joseph. Luke writes, for example, that Joseph 'went to be registered with

---

[1]Matthew 1.19–21, 24–25.
[2]Matthew 2.11.
[3]Matthew 2.13.
[4]Matthew 2.14, 20.
[5]Matthew 2.22–23.
[6]Luke 1.27, 2.4, 16.
[7]Luke 2.33.

Mary' and not, as one might have read in Matthew, that Joseph 'took Mary to be registered', as if she were a dependant – and dependent on him.[8] Mary and Joseph are together with Jesus when the shepherds arrive[9] and both Joseph and Mary hear and marvel at Simeon's prophecy.[10]

The Gospel of Luke also *celebrates* Mary's role in his account of the birth of Jesus. Gabriel visits Mary and tells her not only that her elderly relative Elizabeth had conceived but also that Mary was to conceive through the Holy Spirit.[11] Luke recounts Mary's visit to Elizabeth[12] and her hymn of praise and rejoicing ('the Magnificat').[13] He highlights Mary's godly response to Gabriel,[14] a response that is in marked contrast to Zechariah's earlier response,[15] as well as her reflective attention to what the shepherds say.[16] He highlights her special place in what God purposed by describing her as having God's grace[17] and being 'blessed among women'.[18]

Why are there so many marked differences, not of fact but of approach and focus, between the Gospels of Matthew and Luke?

---

[8]Luke 2.5.
[9]Luke 2.16. Compare this with Matthew 2.11 when the Magi arrive.
[10]Luke 2.33.
[11]Luke 1.26–38.
[12]Luke 1.39–56.
[13]Luke 1.46–55.
[14]Luke 1.38.
[15]Luke 1.11–20.
[16]Luke 2.19.
[17]Luke 1.28, 30.
[18]Luke 1.42

Cultural background clearly plays a part. Matthew was almost certainly from a Jewish background. Palestinian Judaism, which is probably the Judaism of Matthew, was more conservative than the Judaism of other parts of the Roman Empire. In Palestinian Judaism, patriarchy (the legal and social dominance of men) is the underlying model of relationships. The principal role of women would be in the home and family and, because of the way the Levitical laws of purity were interpreted (particularly with regard to menstruation), women took almost no part in the Temple and synagogue. Not surprisingly and as we have seen, this model of relationships and roles is evident in Matthew's account of the birth of Jesus.

In contrast, Luke was a Gentile (non-Jew) who had been influenced by the Hellenism (Greek thought and culture) of the Roman Empire. Hellenistic culture was also patriarchal, though less so than in Palestinian Judaism. What we can say is that, in contrast to what is characteristic in Palestinian Judaism, the role of women was not confined to the home and family, and women had many more legal advantages.

The differences of approach and focus also have to do with the intended audience of the Gospels.

Matthew is writing a Gospel for a Jewish-Christian audience and he writes to show that Jesus came from a conventional Palestinian Jewish background. Much of the rest of the Gospel shows Jesus also rooted in Palestinian Judaism. Jesus is sometimes critical of that Palestinian Judaism and, when he gives the commission to take the gospel to the entire world, he sets the Judaism from which he came on a course that in its later expressions transcended its Palestinian roots.

Luke's interests are different. He has a great heart for down-trodden people and for those who were oppressed or disadvantaged. We see this repeatedly in his Gospel. In Mary's own words in the Magnificat, the proud, the powerful and the rich will be thwarted and even opposed by God.[19] The 'poor' (shorthand for those who were powerless and dominated) will be favoured. So 'lowly' Mary received grace[20] and Israel (here meaning the oppressed people of God) would be sure to receive God's help.[21]

If we read the birth accounts in the Gospel of Luke carefully, we see how this is illustrated. Godly but childless Elizabeth conceives and says that God 'took away the disgrace' of being childless.[22] In contrast, Gabriel strikes dumb her husband Zechariah, a member of the priestly caste and so among the 'haves' rather than the 'have-nots'.[23] Mary, a young girl who conceived without the agency of a man and endured the social stigma that went with an unmarried woman's pregnancy, has a central place in

---

[19]Luke 1.51–53.
[20]Luke 1.48. See 1.52.
[21]Luke 1.54.
[22]Luke 1.25.
[23]Luke 1.20.

the story. She received 'favour' from God (the word in Greek is 'grace').[24] The shepherds (of low social significance), godly (but otherwise unknown) Simeon and the devout and elderly widow Anna, all received angelic or prophetic revelations about Jesus. Note that those who were at the centre of power and influence do *not* feature: the high priests, the teachers of the law, the scribes and the Pharisees.

From these brief observations, we see that it is important to read each of the Gospels in its socio-cultural context *and*, as we saw in the reflection headed 4 December, as separate books with distinct theological emphases, purposes and focuses. When it comes to the birth accounts, we often mix and muddle what is in Matthew and Luke, and if we do that, we lose the clarity of the voice of each of Matthew and Luke. We can also fall into the trap of mishandling and misapplying their writings, because we fail to see them in their context and so fail to interpret and apply them appropriately.

We can draw some practical observations from each of the Gospels.

In Matthew, we have a godly, honourable husband to Mary who obediently and in faith yields to God. In response to God, he married his pregnant fiancée (despite his initial reluctance) and without demur fled first to Egypt and then to Galilee, where

---

[24]Luke 1.28, 30.

he and his family settled. His life and faith are an example for the people of God today.

No doubt, as Joseph obeyed God, he was sometimes puzzled and even fearful, especially as life became hard when he fled with his family from Bethlehem. He probably wondered whether he had rightly understood what God had told him to do. At times, he may have felt like giving up and ignoring his young son's need for safety. Nevertheless, he continued to listen to God and to yield to God.

This has implications for us. Doing God's will is not necessarily easy or straightforward. In Joseph's case, we have the benefit of hindsight and historical perspective that Joseph did not. If God calls us to take steps of faith, we too should not necessarily expect to understand why God asks us to do it. We should also not assume that the process of being obedient will be comfortable and pleasant or that the effects of obedience will be uncomplicated.

In Luke, the focus is not on Joseph but on Mary, and her obedience to God. As a young woman who was an unmarried mother in the first century, she is an example of those who may be easily despised, ignored and underestimated. God gives her grace and a unique role as the mother of God's son that challenge preconceptions and confronts judgementalism. Though a woman, she sees angels, receives angelic announcements and prophesied in the Magnificat. By choosing Mary, God reversed the pattern of expectations that most people would have, and worked in unanticipated ways through an apparently unlikely person.

Mary's life and faith, like Joseph's in the Gospel of Matthew, are an example for the people of God today. They demonstrate that God 'gives grace to the humble' (1 Peter 5.5). That means that God gives grace to women, as well as to men, and grace in at least equal measure.

It is easy to fall into the trap of thinking that the less prepossessing will receive less of God's favour. The opposite is true. God has a heart for the downtrodden and disparaged, and compensates them with an added measure of grace because they lack what others have. As David Sheppard famously wrote as the title of a book, God has a 'bias to the poor'.[25]

In our own discipleship we can seek to help redress the unfair disadvantage that some people face today. By doing this, we model the gospel and we will ourselves receive grace from God.[26]

---

[25]Published in 1983 (London: Hodder & Stoughton).
[26]2 Corinthians 9.6–15.

DECEMBER 7

Christmas . . . and prophecy

In the past, God spoke in many different ways to our forebears through the prophets. Latterly, he has spoken to us through a son.

HEBREWS 1.1

Have you ever thought about how God communicates with people?

The writer to the Hebrews says that, in the period before Jesus, God used many different ways to speak to people.[1] One of the principal ways was by prophets.

We know that in the Old Testament prophets spoke words in the form of direct speech from God. These words could be either about the future ('foretelling') or to give a new perspective or insight into a current situation ('forthtelling').

---

[1] Hebrews 1.1.

On other occasions, prophets acted out their prophetic messages by symbolic actions. For example, Hosea married a prostitute as an illustration of Israel's faithlessness. He had children by her and the names given to the children were strikingly unusual. When interpreted, the names amounted to warnings to the people of Judah about coming judgement.[2] Another example (which seems strange to modern people) is Isaiah's prophetic action: God called him to take off his outer garments and sandals and to go about 'stripped' or 'exposed' (perhaps even 'naked') for 3 years. When explained, his actions amounted to a warning to the Jews that to rely on the political and military help of Egypt and Ethiopia against the Assyrians was misplaced. Soon, like captives in war, the Jews would be led away defeated, and so naked and ashamed.[3]

Prophecy has an important place in the accounts of the birth of Jesus.

Matthew quotes from Old Testament prophecies that he believed 'foretold' the birth of Jesus and the events surrounding his birth. In fact, he quotes prophecy at every significant point in his account: the virginal conception, Jesus' birth in Bethlehem, the escape to Egypt, Herod's massacre of the boys in Bethlehem and the move to Nazareth.[4] For Matthew, nothing

---

[2]See Hosea 1.2–11 and 3.1–5.
[3]Isaiah 20.1–6.
[4]See Matthew 1.22, 2.5, 15, 17 and 23.

to do with the birth of Jesus happened by chance. God anticipated the events (perhaps even ordered them) and integrated
them into a coherent plan for salvation.

To a modern reader, the way Matthew interprets prophetic
texts is odd and we would say, if we follow a modern approach
to interpretation, that his quotations are sometimes out of context and do not support the interpretation and application he
gives them.

However, Matthew used an accepted pattern of interpretation that other Jewish interpreters followed at the time. To
Matthew's mind, the ancient prophecies had a meaning that
fitted their contemporary context (this is unexceptional) *and* a
meaning that applied to other situations that have no obvious
link to the prophecies.[5] In effect, Matthew implies that, with
the benefit of hindsight, the prophecies he quotes, whatever else
they may have been referring to, also refer to Jesus' birth.

When it comes to the Gospel of Luke, there is an altogether
different approach.

Luke does not refer to prophecies from the Old Testament to
explain the events of Jesus' birth. Instead, he quotes *contempo-
raneous* prophetic utterances to interpret those events and to set
them in their wider context.

---

[5]Paul has the same idea about the purpose of prophecy and the Old Testament in
general. He says in Romans 15.4 that 'what was written in former days was for *our*
instruction'.

Luke refers to four people who prophesied: Mary, Zechariah, Simeon and Anna.[6] The prophecies that these people uttered explained what God would do through both John the Baptist and Jesus.

In addition, though strictly speaking not prophecies, utterances by angels have an important part in explaining the meaning and purpose of Jesus' birth. Gabriel speaks to Zechariah[7] and to Mary.[8] An unnamed angel speaks to the shepherds and then the shepherds hear 'a multitude of the heavenly host' praising God.[9]

The differences between Matthew's and Luke's approaches can probably be explained when we realize why and for whom each of them was writing.

We have seen that almost certainly Matthew was writing to a primarily Jewish-Christian church.[10] Its members were seeking to understand how their Christian faith had its roots in the Jewish traditions from which they had come, and, as we shall see in the reflection headed 19 December, how Gentiles could be included in the Christian Church. This helps to explain

---

[6]Luke 1.46–55, 68–79, 2.29–32, 34 and 2.38. We often refer to Luke 1.46–55, 1.68–79 and 2.29–32 as 'the Magnificat', 'the Benedictus' and 'the Nunc Dimittis' respectively. These titles are the first words of these passages in Latin.

[7]Luke 1.13–17, 19–20.

[8]Luke 1.28, 30–33 and 35–37.

[9]Luke 2.10–12, 14.

[10]See the reflection headed 4 December.

Matthew's interest in and focus on Old Testament prophecy. From his viewpoint, it *foretold* Jesus' birth.

In contrast (and also as we have seen),[11] Luke seems to have been writing primarily for a church of Gentiles (non-Jews). The Lukan Gentiles were more interested to know what Jesus' birth meant, rather than how it was rooted in Old Testament prophecy. Hence, Luke focused on prophecy and angelic utterances that *explain* Jesus' birth. He shows that it rested in long-held Jewish expectations and had to be interpreted in that context.

Why is prophecy so important in the accounts of the birth of Jesus in Matthew and Luke?

I suggest the reason is that Matthew and Luke each want to show that God's plan for the world through Jesus was in place *before* Jesus fulfilled that plan. What happened at the first Christmas was not haphazard, or coincidental, or luck, or chance. Nor was it that God was 'making it up as he went along'. Rather, what happened was by the intention of God and that at various times, prophetic messages anticipated, explained and set out that intention. Consequently, whether one looked back to former prophecies (as Matthew did) or let new prophecies explain what was happening (as Luke did), the prophecies indicate that God's long-held intentions were being fulfilled and that God was playing an active part in all human

---

[11]In the reflection headed 4 December.

history. Events that appear to be random are therefore not in fact random at all.

Many theologians infer from this that, in the period after Jesus, God *remains* at work in human affairs. What happens today does not happen by chance or haphazardly, even when it feels like it or appears that way.[12] As one hymn says, God continues to work out his purposes 'as year succeeds to year'.[13]

Yet the picture is more complex. In ways that we do not (and cannot) understand, God not only sometimes orders human affairs and what we do but also interlaces his plans and purposes with the *freedom* we each have to make independent choices.[14] We are free and independent, even to make wrong choices or to do evil.

This undoubtedly introduces an element of chance and unpredictability into the world and human affairs. On the one hand, we are not robots, controlled by God to carry out his purposes. We are free to make good choices or to be foolish and do wrong. On the other hand, we are not detached from what God purposes, as if living in a world from which God is absent and in which God has no say. God *is* active in human affairs and in us, and creation

---

[12]For example, Romans 8.28–39.

[13]The first line of the hymn is *God is working his purpose out as year succeeds to year* by Millicent Kingham.

[14]Our freedom is, of course, limited by our own upbringing, society's conditioning, and so on. No one is entirely free from all constraints. This does not take away from the point I am making that we are not compelled by God to act in certain ways and that we have a significant measure of choice about what we do or do not do.

is more than an arbitrary configuration of atoms and molecules, governed by chance, caprice or human decisions.

These observations are paradoxical, and it is not possible, from our perspective, to reconcile the fact that we are both free to make choices and that God can be actively involved in ordering the way things are. We have to live in the knowledge of both aspects of this paradox. We see the paradox illustrated in the way Jesus *did* fulfil God's plan and the prophecies made about him, despite the fact that his freedom of choice (and the freedom of choice of others) also introduced enormous risks and uncertainties as to whether what God purposed *would* be fulfilled.

Two implications at least follow from today's reflection.

The first is that we can rest in confidence that God's intentions will ultimately be fulfilled, even if human folly appears to get in the way and apparently thwart what we understand to be the will of God.

The second is that in making choices about how to live and what to do, we should have an eye on what we understand to be the will of God. This means we should ensure that our actions and reactions cohere with what we understand to be God's intentions for men and women. To lie, cheat, covet, destroy and harm others are not what God would have us do.

If you are not sure what it means in practice to live God's way, a simple starting point is to act lovingly. If we strive to do this, we are not likely to go wrong.

Christmas . . . and Zechariah

Zechariah was filled with the Holy Spirit and prophesied.

LUKE 1.67

We now begin a series of reflections about the birth of Jesus and about events and people associated with his birth. As best we can, we consider the events in the order they happened, though there is some overlap, as you will see.

This reflection is about Zechariah, the father of John the Baptist.

We do not often pay much heed to Zechariah. This is not surprising, since Advent is primarily about preparing to celebrate the birth of Jesus. Even so, Zechariah is an integral part of the story of the birth of Jesus in the Gospel of Luke, and it is worth spending some time turning our minds to what Luke says about him.

Zechariah was a Levite who served as a priest in the Temple. His principal duties would have been to help with the daily sacrifices, when the group of priests of which he was a member was on duty. (There were 24 such groups, and Zechariah was a member of the eighth group, called 'the division of Abijah'.)

Besides offering sacrifices, priests did other tasks from time to time when their group was on duty. One such task was to offer incense at the Table of Incense in the Holy Place in the Temple.

Priests offered incense twice a day (morning and evening) as part of the routine of the daily sacrifice. Luke says that priests were chosen by lot to make the incense offering.[1] To offer incense was a rare opportunity for a priest. Joachim Jeremias has calculated that a priest would have the opportunity to offer incense at the Table of Incense probably no more than twice in his lifetime.[2]

It was a great privilege to offer incense. This was because the Table of Incense stood immediately in front of the curtain that screened the Holy Place (where the Table of Incense was positioned) from the Holy of Holies. People believed that God's presence was in the Holy of Holies, behind the curtain. So if a priest offered incense at the Table of Incense, he would be, with one exception only, as close as anyone could be to the Holy of Holies and to the presence of God. (The exception was that the

---

[1]Luke 1.9.
[2]*Jerusalem in the Time of Jesus* (London: SCM, 1969), p. 200.

High Priest was allowed once a year to enter the Holy of Holies on the Day of Atonement.)

In Luke's account of Jesus' birth, it was Zechariah's turn to offer incense in the Temple. It was therefore a very special occasion for Zechariah. It was also an opportunity that might not recur in his lifetime.

To put it bluntly, Zechariah made a spectacular mess of the occasion.

While Zechariah was concentrating hard on offering incense, the archangel Gabriel appeared to Zechariah. Zechariah was so focused on what he was doing and on its importance that he was, I suspect, thrown when interrupted. He was all the more thrown because it was an angel interrupting him.

Two thoughts may have gone through Zechariah's mind. The first was that it was more important to offer the incense properly than to listen to Gabriel; the second was that Gabriel would be angry with him if he became distracted from the task in hand. I think he was wrong on both counts.

It is easy for those engaged in Christian ministry to become focused on the mechanics of what they are doing, honourable and proper though those mechanics may be, and to miss God speaking. If one is undertaking something special, unique, difficult or complex, it is especially easy to lose sight of why and for whom one is doing the task and to forget that the primary purpose of what one is doing are not the mechanics of the task in hand but the aim or end to which the task is directed.

Undeterred by Zechariah's reaction, Gabriel said that Elizabeth, Zechariah's wife who had not mothered a child and who by then was well past the age of childbearing, would give birth to a son, who was to be named 'John'.

Zechariah seems to have responded irritably, querulously and sceptically. He was probably a hard-nosed man who carried with difficulty the disappointment that he and Elizabeth were childless.[3] He therefore asked for a sign that what Gabriel said *would* happen, as he was doubtful it *could* happen, given his age and the age of Elizabeth. Gabriel pointed out to Zechariah that his response was one of unbelief, and said that the only sign he would be given was that he would be dumb until the prophecy was fulfilled.[4]

True to Gabriel's word, Zechariah was dumb when he came out from the Holy Place. When the people saw Zechariah, they realized, probably from Zechariah's troubled look, that Zechariah had seen a vision. They realized something was amiss. Zechariah tried to explain by gesticulating but, because he could not also speak, he could not make himself clear.[5]

---

[3]'Curmudgeonly' is the word I want to use about Zechariah but Melanie insists that this is too obscure to use!
[4]Luke 1.20.
[5]Luke 1.22.

What humiliation for Zechariah!

As the weeks went by, one can imagine him replaying in his mind what he had said and done and what he *should* have said and done instead. Because he was dumb, he could not even talk to others about what he thought and felt. (If you have ever tried to communicate your thoughts and feelings not by speaking but by writing on paper, you will understand Zechariah's difficulties.) He may also have wished that Gabriel had appeared to him in a private setting so that his foolish response to the angel and its consequences would not have been so publicly evident.

There are times when Christians fail, and fail spectacularly. The failure can be public or it can be failure in secret, known only to the person concerned. The failure can be bitter, destructive and, at times, self-consuming.

Many of us want to give up in embarrassment and shame when we have failed.

That is not the right response.

The right response, I believe, is to keep going. Winston Churchill once said, 'Failure is not fatal. Success is not final. It is the courage to continue that counts.'

This is true in a secular context; it is certainly also true for Christians, because God does not give up on those who fail.

An example of someone who failed yet had the courage to go on was Peter. Even though he had been full of brash self-confidence, he denied that he knew (or had even met) Jesus when questioned after Jesus had been arrested.[6] He was frightened when confronted and was unable to face the threat that being linked with Jesus presented.

One senses Peter's pain and shame about this when, after the resurrection, Jesus asked Peter three times if Peter loved him.[7] Yes, of course, Peter did, despite his failure to show it when earlier he had denied Jesus, also three times. In saying that he did love Jesus, Peter may also have wondered how Jesus could ever love and trust him again.

Peter did not give up on Jesus.[8] More importantly, Jesus did not give up on Peter. Jesus continued to love and accept Peter. Jesus also gave Peter a central role in the formation of the early Church. Peter's failure was not fatal. What counted was his courage to go on, despite his former failure. By going on, Peter was able to experience God's forgiveness, restoration and grace.

Another example is from the period of the Old Testament.

Israel's persistent failure to live as God had directed led to captivity, first in Assyria (for ten of the tribes) and then in Babylon (for the remaining two tribes, Judah and Benjamin). The apparently impossible had happened: God's people, who thought they had been given forever the land that had been promised to Abraham, forfeited that land because of their unbelief and sin. It was public disgrace for the people of God.

---

[6]Mark 14.66–72.
[7]John 21.15–17.
[8]John 21.7.

It also seemed to be disgrace for the God of Israel, who, in the eyes of Israel's captors, apparently had not been able to rescue the people from captivity and exile.

In an Old Testament book called 'Lamentations', Jeremiah wrote about the crushing sense of despair brought on by the catastrophe of the exile in Babylon for the two tribes. It is one of the saddest and most depressing books in the Old Testament . . . until one gets to a pivotal point in chapter 3. At that point,[9] Jeremiah discloses how he regains perspective. He says, 'This I call to mind and therefore I have hope' and then sets out the grounds of his confidence. The grounds are that God's love is unwavering and unceasing, that God's mercies are unending and renewed daily and that God's loyalty to his people is immeasurable.[10] This gave Jeremiah courage to look forward and to face the future.

What about Zechariah in Luke's account?

He remained dumb until the point when his newborn child was named 'John', as Gabriel had directed, and not 'Zechariah', as Elizabeth and Zechariah's neighbours and relatives expected. When the child was named, the prophecy about John's birth and naming were fulfilled and, as Gabriel had promised, Zechariah spoke again.

It is likely that the chastening Zechariah experienced had reshaped him. The chastening had been for Zechariah's good

---

[9]Lamentations 3.21.
[10]Lamentations 3.22–23.

and, as the writer of the letter to the Hebrews says in another context, had produced, I suspect, 'holiness' and 'the peaceful fruit of righteousness'.[11] The result was that Zechariah did not irritably grumble about what had happened to him. Rather, he was filled with the Holy Spirit and prophesied in words that have come to us in what we now call 'the Benedictus'.[12]

Zechariah's failure, though bitter, was not fatal. God was still at work despite Zechariah's initial scepticism and unbelief. Out of Zechariah's failure has come a hymn of praise that millions of people say or sing as part of their corporate and private worship. God did not give up on Zechariah and Zechariah did not need to give up on God. After failure, there was renewal and restoration.

Which failures do you remember with shame and embarrassment? Have you given up or backed away as a result? Or are you so bruised that you are now afraid to step out in confident faith?

Perhaps now is the time to call to mind God's unwavering love, mercy and loyalty for all people, including those who think they have failed or are failures, so that, like Zechariah, you may be renewed and restored.[13] With God, there is always the opportunity of a new start, no matter what we have previously done.

---

[11]Hebrews 13.10–11.

[12]Luke 1.68–79.

[13]We may also need to put right with other people wrongs we have done to them as part of the way we turn back to God. This is called 'repentance' and is an important step that precedes person-to-person forgiveness. See Anthony Bash, *Just Forgiveness* (London: SPCK, 2011), pp. 20–25.

Christmas . . . and Elizabeth

Both Zechariah and Elizabeth were righteous in the sight of God. They lived blamelessly, following all the Lord's commandments and regulations.

LUKE 1.6

Elizabeth's story is interwoven not only with the story of Zechariah but also with the story of Mary and her pregnancy. We cannot recount Elizabeth's story on its own; it is part of a pattern of events in which others also share. Her story makes sense only when seen in the context of those other stories.

Our own lives may be like that too. Where I am today, what sort of a person I am, whom I know, where I work and my social relationships are all part of a bigger picture in which others have had a part, sometimes for good . . . and sometimes for not so good.

Elizabeth, like her husband Zechariah, came from the tribe of Levi. Luke says that both she and Zechariah were godly, and they kept the Jewish law and feared God.[1]

As we saw when we thought about Zechariah, Elizabeth had not been able to have children. Zechariah had prayed earnestly for a child.[2] Probably, so too had Elizabeth, though we are not specifically told that she had. Despite the prayers, Elizabeth had not conceived. At the time when Luke begins his Gospel, both Elizabeth and Zechariah were too old to have children.

Being childless carried a social stigma for a woman. Elizabeth regarded her childlessness as a 'disgrace' in the community.[3] Childlessness was also a religious issue, because it was apparently a sign of being cursed by God for being godless and evil.[4]

Elizabeth and Zechariah therefore faced a difficulty. Though they kept the law and pleased God, they had not experienced the blessings of God as they had expected, and as their community had expected. They also had to face an additional difficulty: their prayers for a child were unanswered.

Walking with God and living in obedience to him does not guarantee a happy, successful or easy life. I believe God *does* bless those who love and fear him, but that does not mean that

---

[1] Luke 1.6. To 'fear' God does not mean they were 'afraid' of God; it means they reverently worshipped God.
[2] Luke 1.13.
[3] Luke 1.25.
[4] See, for example, Psalms 127, 128 and Deuteronomy 28.4, 18.

God will bless them in the way they expect or at the time they expect. Job had to face this dilemma, and so did Asaph (as Psalm 73 so powerfully sets out).

If we face such a situation, we may need what Paul calls 'the spirit of faith'.[5] This helps us to look at the present with eternity in mind. The blessing God gives may not be evident today, tomorrow or the day after; it may not even be evident in our lifetime. That does not mean there is not a blessing; it means only that it does not come at the time we expect.

As for apparently unanswered prayer, I find it best to think in this way. There is no certainty that God will answer our prayers in the way we want or at the time that we want. I believe God *does* answer every prayer. It is with one of three answers: either 'Yes' or 'No' or 'Wait'.

We return to the story of Elizabeth.

As we read in the previous reflection, an angel, Gabriel, told her husband that she would conceive, despite her age. That did happen. Elizabeth hid herself for 5 months, until the pregnancy became obvious.

The fact that Elizabeth conceived and the fact that she conceived after an angel said that she would become pregnant have echoes of two similar stories in the Old Testament. Sarah, wife of Abraham, conceived when she was long past the age

[5] 2 Corinthians 4.13.

of childbearing[6] and Hannah conceived after pouring out her heart in prayer to God.[7]

Both these women gave birth to children who were significant in Israel's history. Sarah gave birth to Isaac, who was the first of Abraham's lineal descendants whom God promised to bless; Hannah gave birth to Samuel, the last of the judges and the first of the prophets.

Gabriel told Zechariah that the child Elizabeth was to carry would have an important place in Israel's history. The child, when grown up, was 'to make ready a people prepared for the Lord'.[8] Years later, Jesus also speaks of the significance of the child (then known as 'John the Baptist'), and says of him that none was greater than he.[9] Elizabeth would have known what Gabriel had told Zechariah about John's important future role.

At this point, Luke now tells us about *Mary's* miraculous pregnancy. (We think about her pregnancy in the reflection headed 11 December.) He says that Gabriel appeared to *Mary* and told Mary that *she* would conceive. He also told Mary that Elizabeth, her relative,[10] was pregnant. In response, Mary went to visit Elizabeth as quickly as she could, probably because she was delighted to hear this news about Elizabeth and because

---

[6]Genesis 17.15–21, 18.9–15 and 21.1–7.
[7]1 Samuel 1.1–20.
[8]Luke 1.17.
[9]Luke 7.28.
[10]Luke 1.36.

she knew that Elizabeth would understand her own difficult situation.

It is important to realize that when Mary arrived at Elizabeth's house, Elizabeth did not know that Mary was already pregnant, or how she had become pregnant, or that she was carrying the long-awaited Messiah.

Before Mary could explain and immediately after she had no more than greeted Elizabeth, the child in Elizabeth's womb 'leaped for joy'. Luke implies Elizabeth's child was acknowledging, perhaps even rejoicing about, the child Mary was carrying. Elizabeth herself was filled with the Holy Spirit and prophesied. In the prophecy, she affirmed that Mary was carrying the 'Lord'. She probably realized then that, though *her* son was to be significant in what God purposed, Mary's son would have a greater place.

This simple realization would have had some important implications for both Mary and Elizabeth.

In communities at that time, status was all-important. Those of low status were expected to pay respect to and honour those of higher status. It was important to know where one stood in the 'pecking order' so that one could appropriately play one's part. Age was an important way of measuring status, and (in the absence of other factors) older people were usually regarded as having higher status because of their age.

It was not therefore surprising that Mary chose to visit Elizabeth, because Mary was the younger woman visiting a housebound and pregnant older relative.

Even so, *Elizabeth* became surprised that Mary should be visiting her.[11] This is because the child Mary was carrying was of higher status (because given a more exalted role in what God purposed) than the child Elizabeth was carrying. In these circumstances, and despite Elizabeth's years of chronological seniority, convention would have insisted that Elizabeth visit Mary, and not vice versa.

God *could* have told Elizabeth to visit Mary, in conformity to social customs, but God did not.

Should this surprise us? I do not think so. The gospel challenges and undermines many of our social conventions and reverses the accepted social status. It insists, for example, that the first (those of high social status) will be last (of low social status) and the last will be first.[12] It requires us to treat people (such as children and social outcasts) for who they are, and not according to their supposed low status. It insists that leaders are to serve rather than to be served.

I have one more observation to make from the story of Elizabeth.

Even though Elizabeth knew that her child would be 'great in the eyes of the Lord',[13] she readily accepted that her child's role would be subordinate to the role of Mary's child. There is not even a hint that she was disappointed that her child would play

---

[11]Luke 1.43.
[12]Luke 13.30, Matthew 20.16, for example.
[13]Luke 1.15.

'second fiddle' to her younger relative's child; neither is there a hint that she forced him into a role that God had not laid out for him.

Those of us with children want the best for our children, and sometimes that means that we press them to play a part that neither suits them nor fits with what God would have them do. All too often, we hope our children will live out our own unfulfilled expectations or ambitions, or we map out for our children a path that is different from the path our children want or follow.

Elizabeth does not appear to have made mistakes such as these, but accepted what God had set out for her child.

We do not know whether Elizabeth knew that this would mean that her son would live frugally in the desert preaching an uncompromising and (with some) unpopular message, that he would be imprisoned and that he would be brutally executed to satisfy the malicious whim of a bitter woman.[14]

If we have children, we should help them to find (and fulfil) the place and role that God has given them if we can and if they let us. If our children yield to God in that way, we should rejoice, even if the place and role are not what we would have chosen.

Who knows who may benefit as a result?

---

[14]See Matthew 14.1–12 and Mark 6.14–29.

Christmas . . . and forgiveness

You will go before the Lord to prepare his paths
to give knowledge of his salvation
through the forgiveness of sins.

LUKE 1.76, 77

As we have seen in the two previous reflections, Elizabeth, wife of Zechariah the priest, conceived and gave birth to a child in her senior years, long after losing all hope of having a baby.

Shortly after the birth of their son, John, and before Jesus was born, Zechariah 'was filled with the Holy Spirit'[1] and miraculously prophesied about John (who would be called 'prophet of the Most High')[2] and about the saviour of Israel, whose way John was to prepare.

---

[1]Luke 1.67.
[2]Luke 1.76.

Zechariah's prophecy refers to 'salvation' and to the 'forgiveness of sins', that is, forgiveness of the wrongs that people do.[3] This reflection is about what 'forgiveness' in the phrase 'the forgiveness of sins' means. In academic circles, there is considerable debate about whether it was John's baptism that brought about the forgiveness of sins, or whether it was Jesus himself, whose way John was preparing.

I come down firmly on the side that it was Jesus, and Jesus alone, through whom forgiveness of sins comes. For the rest of this reflection, I will assume that is the case.[4]

In the prophecy, Zechariah is pointing to the heart of the gospel by saying that Jesus would bring salvation through the forgiveness of sins.

At the root of the word 'forgiveness' is the idea of release or letting go. What Zechariah is saying is that, in saving people, God releases people from their sins.

This has a twofold meaning.

First, God releases people from the continuing power that sin may have over their lives. Paul makes much of this in Romans,[5] and says that sin no longer enslaves us. The Holy Spirit, who lives in all Christians, strengthens and helps them to resist temptation and so to resist sin.

---

[3]Luke 1.77.

[4]If you want to know more about the arguments and the reasons for my conclusion, see *Forgiveness and Christian Ethics* (Cambridge: Cambridge University Press, 2007) and *Just Forgiveness* (2011), both by Anthony Bash.

[5]For example, in chapters 6 and 8.

That does not mean that we become free of sin as Christians. All too many people can tell, sometimes with much pain and sadness, about their continuing struggle to say 'no' to sin (and to particular sins) and about what, for them, can be repeated failure to live as they know they ought.

Secondly, God releases us from the consequences of sins, in the sense that God no longer holds them against us. By fully entering into the human condition, Jesus 'was made sin' for us[6] and in dying, died for that sin representatively for us. We now share his resurrection life and can rejoice that 'there is now no condemnation' for those who share in his death and rising.[7]

The word that we translate as 'forgiveness' means rather more than 'release from sins'. It refers to 'release' in a much wider sense. It refers, in fact, to the whole scope and range of God's restorative work through the cross and the ministry of Jesus.

We see this clearly in Luke 4.16–21, when Jesus spoke one Sabbath in the synagogue at Nazareth, his hometown. He quoted from Isaiah 61.1–2 that he clearly regarded as being about himself and the work God had called him to do. In Luke 4.18, he refers to 'release' for captives and to 'freedom' for the oppressed. The words that are translated 'release' and 'freedom' are from the same word that is elsewhere translated 'forgiveness'.

---

[6] 2 Corinthians 5.21.
[7] Romans 8.1. See also the reflection headed 24 December.

To release, to free and to forgive are at the heart of what Jesus came to do. The effect of the release, freedom and forgiveness is on individuals personally and on communities. It will also be on all the created order, for God will make 'a new heaven and a new earth'.[8] The natural world as we now know it, 'groaning in decay' according to Paul, will one day be 'freed' (this is the same idea as 'release') and remade.[9] Charles Wesley refers to this in the (now rarely sung) last verse of 'Hark! The herald angels sing' when he writes that Jesus will 'ruined nature now restore'.

Connected with 'release' are the ideas contained in the word 'peace'. 'Peace' refers not only to cessation of hostilities but also to wholeness and healing. Both 'release' and 'peace' are part of the same collection of ideas to do with God freeing people and creation from sin and its destructive effects.

Ideas to do with 'peace' are important in the account of the first Christmas in the Gospel of Luke. 'Peace' is referred to when Zechariah prophesies, when the angels speak to the shepherds and when Simeon blessed God in the Temple.[10] What Luke is pointing his hearers and readers to is that, through Jesus and his work of releasing the world from the effects of sin, God is bringing 'peace' and restoring creation to what it should be.

---

[8]Revelation 21.1.
[9]Romans 8.21.
[10]Luke 1.79, 2.14 and 2.29.

These two ideas, 'release' and 'peace', have practical implications for our lives.

On a *personal* level, we can rejoice that God has forgiven us our sins and does not hold them against us. In consequence, we should seek to live out that forgiveness, striving for personal holiness and to 'put to death' sin.[11] To do this should be our daily aspiration. In practice, this means seeking to love God and other people, and not doing what we know is morally wrong.

On a *social* level, it means, I believe, striving for justice for other people, whether they live in the same country as us, or whether they live abroad. Unjust systems of trade and oppressive governments mean that millions of people are denied economic justice and basic freedoms for day-to-day living. We can be part of God's work of 'release' and 'peace' if we confront these cruel networks that crush people and if we strive for justice.

On an *ecological* level, it means that we should seek to look after the world and its resources, as stewards and not as pillagers. We are 'tenants' of God's world. That means we should leave the world in as good (or preferably better) condition as it was when we came into it.

It is hard to find these themes of personal holiness, social responsibility and ecological stewardship in much of the modern celebration of Christmas. It was certainly not evident in the

---

[11]Romans 8.13.

advertising logo ('Admire, Aspire, Acquire') of a shopping mall that I know.

Perhaps each one of us should ask ourselves three questions.

First, what can we do to put sin to death in our lives? We need to be honest with ourselves and take a critical look at our lives.

Putting sin to death is not an easy or quick process. It is a task that we should enter into prayerfully, seeking the help and enabling of the Holy Spirit and perhaps also the support and encouragement of our friends. It is not wrong to admit to others our sin and our need for help in combating it. I suspect that this is in part what James 5.16 says when James urges us to confess our sins to one another and to pray for one another so 'that we may be healed', that is, released from sin and restored to what we should be.

Secondly, we should ask ourselves how we could translate the gospel into practical actions that are socially responsible and which model the 'release' and 'peace' that are at the heart of the gospel. It is not enough to treat the scope of the gospel as being only about individual sin and personal salvation. The gospel makes demands at a social and political level, and its implications are as great for transforming societal structures as they are for personal renewal. So we must ask ourselves, how can we be involved in modelling God's concern for and engagement with communities so that we promote 'release' (for example, freedom or restoration for the oppressed and downtrodden) and 'peace' (such as wholeness and safety)?

Lastly, we should reflect on how we can care for the world that God has given us so that we nurture it, rather than exploit and ravage it. Small decisions and apparently insignificant choices that individuals make can, if multiplied widely, have an impact for good, both by example and by effect. We should aim to ensure that our use of the world and its resources is not greedy exploitation but respects others' legitimate interests in those resources, whether those people are in this generation or in generations to come.

To celebrate Christmas in a God-honouring way means that we should not neglect holiness that is personal, action that is socially responsible and stewardship that is ecologically wise. Zechariah's prophecy about forgiveness in its broadest sense can help us to renew our commitment to these essential marks of Christian discipleship. Perhaps, we should now begin to think how we can better live out that aspect of discipleship.

Christmas . . . and a girl called Mary

Mary said to the angel, 'Yes. I am God's servant. Let what you have told me now happen.' Then the angel left her.

LUKE 1.38

I still painfully remember one of our children asking me at a school nativity play (in what seemed to be a dreadfully loud voice), 'Daddy, what's a virgin?'

I cannot now remember what my answer was and whether my reply satisfied the curiosity of a 5-year-old child. What I do remember is that it struck me at the time that what happened to Mary was awful. I thought that if we had censors for the Bible in the same way that we have censors for films, the story of the 'parthenogenic conception' (that is, the story of Mary's conception of Jesus without Mary having had prior sexual relations) is definitely a PG, if not a 12 or 18!

In the Gospels of Matthew and Luke, it is clear beyond doubt that Mary had not had sexual relations with a man before she became pregnant with Jesus. Luke says twice that Mary was 'a virgin'.[1] Even if one wants to argue that the word 'virgin' might perhaps sometimes mean no more than 'young woman of marriageable age', Luke leaves us in no doubt about what *he* means. He writes that Mary says, 'I do not know a man', meaning, 'I have not had sexual relations with a man.'[2] Matthew makes the same point. He says that Mary was pregnant before she and Joseph had 'come together', meaning that Mary was pregnant without having had a sexual relationship with Joseph.[3] He also says that Joseph 'did not know' Mary until she had given birth to Jesus.[4]

Three aspects of what happened to Mary make it awful.

The first is that Mary was pregnant and not married. Even if to be pregnant and not married were relatively common in the first century (we do not have much evidence to be certain about the frequency of pregnancies to unmarried women), it almost certainly would have had catastrophic effects on Mary's future. Matthew says that Joseph was on the point of ending their relationship (to use modern terminology),[5] which would

---

[1] Luke 1.27.
[2] Luke 1.34.
[3] Matthew 1.18.
[4] Matthew 1.25.
[5] Matthew 1.19.

have forced Mary to continue to live in her parents' home as a single parent.

The second is that Mary was not only pregnant and not married but also, by today's standards, very young. We tend to lose sight of this fact, because many Bible translations refer to Mary as either 'betrothed' (in the older versions) or 'engaged to Joseph' (in modern translations) and so obscure the conventions to do with marriage and courtship that Mary and Joseph were following.

In Jewish customs of the time, many girls were 'betrothed' at about 12 years of age. Though they would continue to live in their family home, they were regarded, for legal purposes, as married. They could therefore be divorced. Sexual relations with a third party in this period of half-marriage were a violation of the marriage contract and one of the grounds of divorce.[6] After about a year, a girl who was betrothed would marry, leave her family home to live with and begin sexual relations with her husband. Typically, a girl would be engaged at 12 and 'wedded and bedded' at 13. In Mary's case, by 12 years of age, she was, almost certainly, legally married to Joseph, still living in her parents' home, pregnant, and without having had sexual relations with Joseph or anyone else.

---

[6]Matthew 1.19 clearly indicates this too.

Lastly, what happened to Mary was awful because Mary knew in *advance* that she would become pregnant without human agency. An angel came to her and greeted her as a 'favoured one' whom the Lord was with, and then told her what was to happen to her.[7]

A favoured one? Someone blessed by the Lord? As little more than a girl, one can only imagine what went through Mary's mind. 'How can I be favoured if it will look as if I have slept around?' she may have wondered. How was she to tell her parents and Joseph? Would they believe her? What would friends and neighbours think? It was as if her aspirations and hopes for the future were dissolving because of God's intervention. For her, life would have become frightening, uncertain, isolating and very risky.

When Mary first heard what Gabriel said to her, she was confused and perplexed.[8] Who would not have been? As she continued to listen, she became more confident. Though she may not have fully understood what was to happen to her or its implications, she accepted what the angel told her.[9]

We often take Mary to be an example of someone who rightly surrenders to the circumstances of her life, and has trust and faith in God. In some traditions, her yielding and

---

[7]Luke 1.28, 30.
[8]Luke 1.29.
[9]Luke 1.38.

submissive response is taken as a paradigm for how women are to respond, even to men who are bullies and cruel. Others suggest it was because Mary yielded to what the angel said (literally, 'Let it be to me according to your word' in Luke 1.38) that God did cause her to become pregnant.

I remain unconvinced that these interpretations are what Luke's account truly indicates, though it is true that Mary's response is a remarkable example of someone who accepted and yielded to God's will.

I suspect that what Luke is pointing to is the fact that Mary *chose wisely how best to respond* when she faced very difficult circumstances. She asked questions as the angel spoke to her and she thought about what was to happen to her. Even though she certainly did not entirely understand the implications of what Gabriel was saying and was, I expect, frightened about what she faced, she trusted that God would sustain her, whatever she faced.

In the months following the meeting with the angel, after she had become pregnant, perhaps she wondered whether she had imagined the encounter. Perhaps she feared and doubted. Even so, she continued to make choices about how to respond wisely and in a godly way to what she saw as the apparent mess of her life. As the accounts of her continuing faith indicate, she believed, though perhaps she did not understand how, that God was with her. She held on to the conviction that, in the context of the wider purposes of God, what was happening made sense, if not to her then to God.

We do not know whether God gave Mary a choice. I suspect Mary would have carried Jesus however she had responded to the angel. The accounts in Luke and Matthew certainly do not indicate that she had a choice about this. She *did* have a choice about how to respond to what she faced. With the hindsight of history, we now see both the wisdom and the significance of Mary's trusting response of faith. I am sure that Mary had had dreams and hopes about what it would be like to be engaged and about what marriage would be like. What happened to her changed those expectations dramatically.

Sometimes, we experience life in the way that Mary did. Something intervenes that changes our hopes for the future. Our goals, our hopes, our longings, the careful plans that we may have laid become impossible, as God reorders the pattern of what our lives now hold. It may be a death, an illness, redundancy, disappointment or something else.

We may rage against God in anger, resenting what has now come to be 'our lot'. We may become bitter and cynical, lamenting our circumstances and looking on others enviously who seem to have none of our disappointment or anguish. Some may become pessimists, assuming that there is no hope for the future and that life will remain inescapably awful. Others may just grit their teeth, internally shutting down so as not to engage with their circumstances.

On the other hand, we may react as Mary did, choosing to trust God, even though we may not understand or welcome the maelstrom we face. We may need the help and encouragement of friends and the working of the Holy Spirit in our lives so that we make godly choices about how we may engage with what we are encountering. Even if we cannot respond as we know we ought, we can admit and acknowledge that, and seek help to change. What matters is that we critically reflect on the options we face and respond as best we can in faith.

Perhaps, like Mary, you are facing tough circumstances. How are you responding? Reflect on the fact that you have choices. You may choose to embrace what God is doing or you may resist. If you yield to God, you are demonstrating that you are practising what it means to live by faith and so to please God.[10] In living by faith in this way, you may discover more about God and the depths of his love. God may also teach you through your circumstances to help others who face difficulties. God does not turn his back on those who, in their difficulties and struggles, yield to him.[11]

---

[10]Hebrews 11.6.
[11]Matthew 11.28–30.

DECEMBER 12

Christmas . . . and children

Zechariah and Elizabeth did not have children because Elizabeth was barren

LUKE 1.7

Mary was found to be carrying a child in her womb from the Holy Spirit.

MATTHEW 1.18

We do not often reflect much about how Elizabeth and Mary may have thought about bearing children.

In the period of the Old Testament and into Jesus' time, it was a 'disgrace' for a woman not to have children.[1] The Bible ascribes the problem of childlessness as due to the 'barrenness' of the

---

[1]Luke 1.25, for example.

woman. In the premedical era, there was no awareness that perhaps the reason could be a male, rather than a female, problem.

When we first read about Elizabeth in Luke 1, I presume that Elizabeth had given up hoping for a child. Though it is nowhere explicitly said, I guess that she grieved for the children she had never been able to carry, and perhaps dwelt on the shame and disgrace that she thought she had brought upon herself and upon her husband.

For women who would like to have a child but have been unable to conceive, it is difficult to convey in words the pain that accompanies childlessness.

An aunt who was unable to have children described the distress of seeing 'buggies and prams everywhere'. When I heard this, I looked around at the world through the eyes of my aunt. I saw that there *were* buggies and prams everywhere, and I also noticed women who were surrounded by *several* children while my aunt had none.

My aunt went on to say that the sadness of childlessness does not end when the children of friends and other family members grow up and leave home. She said that she had not prepared herself for the second wave of sadness that arose when her peers became grandparents. The pain of involuntary childlessness does not end. The ache is often carried through life.

The Old Testament tells us about the pain of labour, but tells us very little about the *experience* of pregnancy. I wonder how Elizabeth felt about being an 'old' pregnant woman.

We know that Elizabeth shut herself away for 5 months. We are not told why. I wonder whether she had 'morning sickness', or feared to lose her much longed for and prayed for child. She may have been embarrassed to be pregnant at her senior age or perhaps she felt God was doing something in and with her that was personal and intimate.

For some women pregnancy can be a wonderful time, when they feel fulfilled, when they feel special to be carrying, growing and nurturing a new and very special life.

For others, pregnancy can be a highly distressing and aversive experience. We have often joked about the silence between women about the horrors of pregnancy, how very few women seem to 'bloom', and that this bloom is often more about a 'blooming awful' experience! The early months of pregnancy are commonly characterized by pathological tiredness that can make normal everyday life impossible. 'Morning sickness' is common, and not just with first pregnancies, not just in the morning, and not just for the first 12 weeks. The hormones that support a pregnancy often lead to marked emotionality and tearfulness.

Some women manage to conceive after much disappointment and unmet hopes. Sometimes, for them, the birth of a child is not necessarily emotionally straightforward or an undiluted joy. We know, for example, that women who carry an IVF pregnancy are at higher than average risk of postnatal depression. This is contrary to what one would expect. Surely, we might think, if the child is much longed for and successfully delivered, delight will follow. However, things that are longed for very rarely meet our (sometimes unrealistic) expectations. Babies do not make us happy all the time. Babies have needs that do not necessarily fit in with our own. They cry at inconvenient times, they fill their nappies at inconvenient times, they become ill and become crotchety. When they are a bit older, they explore their world and learn by tearing apart ours! Being a good parent demands a great deal of selflessness; and most of us are not very good at being selfless all the time. I wonder whether Elizabeth experienced some of these complex, ambivalent feelings.

Did Elizabeth long for a brother or sister for John? The Gospels tell us that Jesus had brothers and sisters. For couples who have been unable to have more than one child and who would have liked more, there is again pain. Children generally like playing with other children, and will often ask for a brother or sister. It can be very difficult for couples to admit that they long for more children but cannot have them. They can often feel poorly understood, even by close friends. 'At least you have one' is the common response. Another friend who was unable to have a third and much wanted child has continued to grieve for the third child she was unable to have, even though she has two very loved children.

I also wonder how Elizabeth might have felt had she lived long enough to know that her longed-for child was killed on a politician's whim in a particularly brutal way to please the politician's wife and daughter. Might Elizabeth have wished that God had called John to be a farmer or labourer or *anything* other than Israel's greatest prophet who lived in a desert and who died in his early thirties?

The other woman with a child in the Christmas story was Mary, a relative of Elizabeth. In contrast to Elizabeth, Mary was pregnant when she had not expected to be, as we saw in the previous reflection.

The disgrace that Mary faced as an unmarried mother is difficult to capture or imagine within today's, Western culture. Yet, it is not so long ago that in the United Kingdom, women were indefinitely locked away in asylums for the 'mentally insane' because they had become pregnant outside marriage.

Mary became pregnant when assuming (if she had thought about it) that it would have been impossible, as she was not sexually active.

For many women for whom a pregnancy is unplanned (as Mary's was), there are often strong feelings of ambivalence. On the one hand, they might feel a strong maternal sense of love towards their unborn child and wish to guard the pregnancy dearly. On the other hand, they may also feel panicked as they reflect on the changes to life that will be introduced by an unplanned child. Some may feel resentful about the bodily changes that are happening to them and the loss of freedom that these bring. Others may grieve for what they anticipate will be the loss of a career or a job and perhaps reduced income. Such ambivalence can induce a sense of guilt with the assumption that it is somehow wrong to hold ambivalence about an unwanted pregnancy.

To use the modern idiom, neither Elizabeth's nor Mary's child were 'planned'. They were gifts from God.

However, I wonder whether it is ever realistic to talk of 'planned' pregnancies? At school, children today are taught in sex education (now called 'Personal and Social Education') that women are fertile around the fourteenth day of their menstrual cycle, and that contraception is effective in avoiding unwanted pregnancies.

Yet many people will testify with deep feeling that pregnancies that result in the birth of a child do not come to order in the way that our education system tells us. Children are not born when we plan or decide. They come when they come, often despite the very best of forethought and family planning. It is often misleading to talk of a pregnancy as being 'planned' or 'not planned'.

Finally, I make some observations that may perhaps surprise you.

Despite the focus on children in the activities of many churches in Advent, children do not feature very much in the New Testament accounts about the first Christmas. The

Christmas story, when read and properly understood, is not principally about children. To suggest that it is distorts the balance of what we have in the New Testament.

Obviously, Jesus' birth is central to the accounts in Matthew and Luke, but we know little about the birth itself or the early years of Jesus.[2] Luke refers to John's birth only incidentally in relation to his parents. Matthew writes of Herod's murderous rage against boys aged 2 and under in the region of Bethlehem. Apart from this, nothing more is said about children.

The focus of the Christmas story in Matthew and Luke is on adults: Elizabeth and Zechariah, Mary and Joseph, shepherds, Magi, Herod, and so on. The fact is that the Christmas story is an *adults' story* principally about *adults*, of whom two gave birth to children with unique roles in history. True, we only have the adults' story because of the children they are connected with; nevertheless, it is a mistake to say that *children* are the focus of the story.

To shape church events and worship around children is to the detriment of *all* people, both adults and children, and misrepresents the theological and literary point of the Christmas story. It also causes unnecessary pain, and even grief, to those who do not have the children they long for. It is important to give *adults* their proper place in the life of the church in Advent.

---

[2]What we have comes only from Matthew and Luke and not Mark and John.

What we need are celebration and reflection that balance the needs of both adults and children. If we overemphasize children in our celebration of Christmas, we run the risk of unhelpfully simplifying the Christmas story. If we neglect adults in our celebration, we face the possibility that adults will be disadvantaged, and left with an impoverished understanding of Advent. Our focus should be the Christmas story as we have it, if we are to become men, women *and* children who live out that story.

DECEMBER 13

Christmas . . . and hardship

Mary gave birth to her first-born son. She wrapped him up to keep him warm. She laid him down in a cattle trough because the lodging houses were full.

LUKE 2.7

Many people have an inbuilt sense that if they live honest, God-fearing, upright lives, God will 'play fair' with them. In practice, such people think that God will shield them from the worst of many of life's blows, and so are surprised, even shocked, when bad things happen to them. A recurring question that people ask is, 'Why do bad things happen to good people?' as well as the inverse of that question, 'Why do so many good things happen to bad people?'

The questions are not new. In many places in the Bible, and in the Old Testament in particular, people wrestled with them.

(The questions have to do with what we now call 'theodicy', the study of why there is so much suffering in a world created by a good God.) Some, such as the writer of Ecclesiastes, despaired and concluded that the world is meaningless, and that doing good or doing evil have no effect on the outcome of their lives and circumstances. Others (such as those of whom we read in Hebrews 11.35–38) resolutely insisted that to live God's way and to do good were always right, and many such people died in appalling circumstances as they held on to their convictions, regardless of the outcomes in the short term. They resisted doing what Job's wife urged Job to do: to curse an apparently uncaring God for their misfortunes and to live as if there were no God.[1]

We saw in the reflection headed 11 December that in all probability it was very hard for Mary to be pregnant by the Holy Spirit when unmarried and aged about 12. We thought about the choices she made in response to her circumstances, and how she responded in a godly way to what she could not change.

After Mary had recovered from the shock of discovering that she was pregnant, she might have thought, if she were perhaps like you or I, that God would treat her favourably. Gabriel had described her as 'the favoured one'.[2] She knew she was carrying 'the Son of the Most High'[3] in whom Israel's longings of

---

[1]Job 2.9.
[2]Luke 1.28.
[3]Luke 1.32.

centuries were to be fulfilled. Might she not have expected 'red carpet' treatment from God, since she had such a significant role in what God was doing for the salvation of humanity and the renewal of creation?

Perhaps she may have hoped for 'red carpet' treatment, but it was not like that at all. In this reflection, we explore some of the events and circumstances that she faced that were far from easy or straightforward.

Shortly before Jesus was to be born, and when Mary was heavily pregnant, Joseph was forced to make a journey from Nazareth to Bethlehem to register at his ancestral place of origin for a census that the Romans had organized. Mary had to go with him because, as his fiancée, she was regarded in law as sharing his domicile of origin.

In the popular mind, Mary travelled by donkey; however, the Gospel of Luke, where the account of the journey is given, does not tell us how she travelled to Bethlehem. Perhaps she walked. By whichever means she travelled, it would have been uncomfortable and painful, and not what someone would have hoped to do immediately prior to giving birth.

Bethlehem was probably teeming with people who had travelled to register. We know that accommodation for visitors was in short supply, because Mary and Joseph were unable to find lodgings. Traditionally, we suppose that Joseph and Mary were unable to find a room in Bethlehem's inn. However, the word that is normally translated 'inn' almost certainly means 'lodgings'. We do not in fact know where they stayed, and I wonder whether it was in the open air.[4]

We popularly suppose that they stayed in a stable (and 'Once in Royal David's City' and 'Away in a Manger' have imprinted this on our minds), though we do not know this for sure. We may perhaps infer that it was a barn because, when the baby was delivered, the baby was put, not in a cot, but in a 'manger', that is, a feeding trough for cattle. Matthew is clear in his Gospel that Jesus was in a 'house', at least at the point when the Magi came,[5] (though Matthew seems unaware that Mary and Joseph were unable to find lodgings in Bethlehem).

Mary would have been without family support as she gave birth and probably without what she needed for a new baby. 'Surely, God', she may have questioned, 'it cannot be right that this child, so special in your purposes, has been born in such awful circumstances and with so little that I need for him?' Perhaps she also murmured to herself when the Magi brought gold, frankincense and myrrh that a Moses basket, a blanket and some clean clothes might have been rather more welcome.

The dislocation that Joseph and Mary faced did not let up. For after Jesus' birth, Joseph and Mary fled to Egypt to avoid

---

[4]The odd way Luke uses the word 'because' in Luke 2.7 seems to imply that where Jesus was put down to sleep was outdoors *because* there was nowhere indoors for Joseph and Mary to stay.
[5]Matthew 2.11.

Herod's murderous intentions against their baby whom Herod saw as a political threat to his power. They remained in Egypt probably for a few months until Herod's death in 4 BC.

The significant role that Mary played in God's plan as the bearer of God's son, a role generally more celebrated in Catholicism (and one which Protestants sometime risk under-estimating), does not mean that to fulfil that role was easy, comfortable or convenient. It was none of these, but was very hard. Her privileged and unique place in the plan of God for humanity's salvation did not mean that God would exempt her from any of life's difficult circumstances; in fact, her special place seems to have been the *cause* of the difficult circum-stances she faced.

There are important principles here for us about disciple-ship. Being a disciple is to 'take up' one's cross,[6] doing not what we necessarily want but what God calls us to do, even if it is hard and not what we would have chosen.[7] Following God means we take up a 'yoke' and a 'burden',[8] living a life some-times with sacrifice and even suffering. We will need courage to persevere, and to persevere with faith. We do not do God a favour following him, and God does not owe us a favour or two (such as an easy life) if we follow him.

---

[6]Luke 9.23.
[7]Luke 22.42.
[8]Matthew 11.30.

We do not know much about Mary's reactions to the difficulties she faced. Certainly, we must be careful not to idealize them. True, her initial reaction to Gabriel in Luke 1.38 was one of godly surrender. Did it always stay that way in the months and years ahead, or did she sometimes 'wobble' in her faith and discipleship? It is not wrong to admit to being afraid about the path God sets for us and about being reluctant to follow that path. Jesus himself did this in the Garden of Gethsemane.[9]

Like all of us, Mary had to face difficulties. I wonder, though, whether *sustained* or *multiplying* difficulties made her dejected and downcast? Were there times when she was weary with following God's pathway and when she longed to be 'an ordinary Mum', living an 'ordinary' life without the privileges and responsibilities God had laid on her?

If we are to stay resolute as disciples, we need to keep in mind the example of men and women of faith in the Bible, as Hebrews 12.1–3, 12–13 urges. It will restore our perspective and help us to keep going. It will stop us from being 'weary' and 'losing heart'. Perhaps, then, we may be able even to sprint to the finishing line God has set for us. Certainly, we will not think that obeying God entitles us to 'red carpet treatment' and end up confused and perhaps disappointed.

---

[9]Matthew 26.36–46, Mark 14.32–42 and Luke 22.40–46.

DECEMBER 14

Christmas . . . and Augustus

Augustus issued a decree that everyone was
to be registered in a census

LUKE 2.1

In the Gospel of Luke, the account of the birth of Jesus is set in the context of the bureaucracy that goes with raising taxes.

Luke refers to an edict made in Rome that a census should be taken in every part of the Roman Empire.[1] Luke says that the edict was issued when Augustus was Emperor (27 BC–AD 14).

The reason for the census was, almost certainly, to identify who was eligible to pay taxes to Rome. Very likely, it took several years to complete the census and the census took place on a piecemeal basis, region by region. It so happened that when

---

[1]Luke 2.1–5.

Mary was pregnant with Jesus, the census for Palestine was being conducted.

We can work out from Luke 2.3 how the census was conducted. People were to be registered in the town of their origin. If they had moved away, they were required to return in order to register.

No doubt, in Rome, where the plans for the census were drawn up, the idea to identify in this way who should pay taxes made good administrative and fiscal sense. No doubt, also, the way the census was to be conducted was efficient from Rome's point of view. I wonder, though, how much thought had been given to the human cost of this bureaucratic decision.

We can see the impact of the way Augustus' edict was implemented in the case of Mary and Joseph.

Joseph originally came from Bethlehem in Judea.[2] It appears he had moved north, to Nazareth in Galilee.[3] We do not know why he had moved. It may have been because there was work in the nearby city of Sepphoris, the capital of Galilee. While Joseph was in Nazareth, he became engaged to a local girl, called Mary.[4]

The consequence of these simple facts that are by no means out of the ordinary is that Joseph had to travel about 90 miles

---

[2] We can infer this from the fact that he had to return to Bethlehem to be registered.
[3] Luke 2.4.
[4] Luke 2.5.

from Nazareth to Bethlehem in order to satisfy Rome's administrative requirements. Even though Mary was from Nazareth, she too had to travel with Joseph and register with him. This is because, as Joseph's fiancée, she was regarded in law as sharing his place of origin. The journey was very difficult for Mary because Mary was in the late stages of pregnancy. As it turned out, she delivered her baby during the period of registration in Bethlehem.

There would have been others who were equally inconvenienced by Rome's requirements, some perhaps even more so. It appears that there were no concessions for those who were pregnant, unable to travel or legitimately committed to other things. One could not register by proxy or in absentia. To us today, and probably also to people at the time, the implementation of Augustus' edict could seem harsh and inflexible. I suspect that Rome would have regarded the human cost of the census to be little more than an unfortunate but necessary cost of the supposed greater good of identifying who should pay taxes to Rome.[5]

God puts a limitation on how civil leaders are to exercise power. In Romans 13.1–7, Paul calls civil leaders 'God's servants',

---

[5]This is akin to the idea of what modern politicians sometimes in warfare call 'collateral damage', that is, the unintended destruction of property and the deaths of innocent civilians as an incidental consequence of military action against enemy combatants and property.

whether or not they are Christians and whether or not they are aware of their God-given role as 'servants'.

Three implications follow from leaders being servants of God.

The first is that leaders are to do what God wants. This is because to be a 'servant' is to be appointed to carry out the wishes of the 'master': a 'servant' is not free to do what he or she wants. In other words, whether or not leaders know this, their role is to act according to the moral framework that God sets out.

The second is that those who have power do not have it by right but they have it because God entrusts it to them. The power is God's power and has its origins in God.[6] Power is only ever lent to people.

Thirdly, those with power are accountable to God for how they use the power God gives them. They may 'get away' with misusing the power when it comes to giving account to people; they will not 'get away' with it with God. I sometimes wonder what measure of judgement will await some of today's leaders who have abused the privileges of the power that God has entrusted to them.

Practically, what are those who have power to do?

I suggest it is to use power as God uses it, that is, above all lovingly. Leaders are to serve those whom they lead or have

---

[6]Romans 13.2.

power over. This means that they should act for the good of those entrusted to them. They should not exercise power selfishly or for their own advancement. Rather, they should exercise power balancing the needs of both the individual and the community. It also means that when leaders exercise power, the 'end' does not necessarily justify the 'means'; the process matters too. In other words, leaders must ensure not only that the outcomes they seek are good and wholesome but also that the processes by which the outcomes are attained are equally good and wholesome.

We do not know what thought went into the edict issued on Augustus' behalf that required the subject-peoples of the Roman Empire to register for tax purposes.

What we do know is that the edict made demands on some people that were harsh and even cruel, and that the edict was implemented apparently without thought for those who would be grievously burdened by it. It was not necessarily that the 'end' was wrong; it was that the 'means' was not loving and sometimes caused great hardship and dislocation.

Most of us exercise power in one situation or another. If you think you are someone who does not exercise any power at all, you are probably mistaken. For example, if you sell cinema tickets, you have a measure of power when you meet the public. If you are treasurer of a local bowls club, you will exercise power in committee meetings. If you are in the sixth form at school, you will have power and influence over younger pupils as well as your peers. The same will be true if you are a manager at work, or a parent or a grandparent. Whoever we are, we will sometimes have power over other people.

Examples such as these are at first sometimes difficult to identify, often because we are reluctant to recognize that we have power and that we exercise power. Yet with a little thought and imagination, examples become easy to multiply and we quickly realize that we all share in complex networks of power. Reflect today on where, when and how you exercise power.

It is wise to reflect anew on how we exercise the power that God has lent us. Are we exercising it in a way that is loving, responsible and honours God? Are there better ways we can exercise that power? Should we also reappraise the processes by which we seek to attain outcomes?

The result may be a transformation of the way we think about what we do. Almost certainly, the way we treat the people we meet and influence will change. The outcome will honour God and be of great benefit to the people we serve.

Christmas . . . and humility

Can anything good come out of Nazareth?

JOHN 1.46

I do not know how to describe this reflection except to say that it is about the humility of God.

As we know, to practise the grace of humility means that we do not put our own needs and preferences first but that instead we consider, and sometimes even put first, others' interests and aspirations. It is to have (and to practise) a balanced and true assessment of ourselves, both in relation to other people and to God. It is to choose not to use power for one's own ends or advancement. It is to seek others' good because they have worth and value as God's children in his image. Someone who models these virtues will eschew selfishness and personal ambition and have in mind the good of the community, even at his or her own expense. They will make themselves vulnerable and appeal to others rather than be insistent, all because they reject self-interest as the determining outlook of their lives.

Most people believe that God is loving, gracious and merciful. They also believe that Jesus lived out these God-like qualities. Reading the Gospels helps us to understand what these qualities mean for us in practice and help us to know and understand God better through them.

Less widely appreciated is that God is also meek and humble. We see this especially in the accounts of the birth of Jesus.

For example, God chose to bring about salvation, forgiveness and reconciliation through Jesus, who was a human being.[1] To be a human being is to face a considerable degree of vulnerability and risk. So, as with you and me, God permitted Jesus to share in the dangerous process of gestation and birth. Like any other human being, he was exposed to diseases that can kill or maim. Like all of us, he faced the risk of death from accidents or crimes. Jesus survived these risks and lived to complete the work that God had set him apart to do. That included yielding to the brutality of a show trial, followed by execution on a trumped-up charge.

In choosing a human being for the work of salvation, God chose a way that gave God (and Jesus) no special privileges, and

[1]Philippians 2.7.

so exemplified what it means to be meek and humble. To put it boldly, God did not trump life's brickbats to ensure Jesus would succeed.

There is another way that we see God's humility exemplified in Jesus.

We read in the reflection headed 11 December that Jesus was carried in the womb of a young girl, aged probably about 12 or 13 years, who was not married. Mary's virginity is emphasized to ensure that we understand that no human agency was involved in the conception of Jesus.[2]

This emphasis had the incidental consequence of importing shame and disgrace on Mary: she was an unmarried mother in the eyes of those who disbelieved that Jesus was conceived without male agency. To put it bluntly, it appeared, to those who were sceptical about Jesus' God-given role, that the mother of Israel's saviour had 'slept around'. Like it or not, there was rather more than a whiff of scandal about Jesus' origins.

Some observers might also have questioned whether Jesus *could* have been the saviour for whom Israel longed, since he had such an apparently doubtful background. Some might say, 'God would not permit the anointed one to be born to a single

---

[2]There are examples of gods fathering children in ancient literature through human mothers, but the idea of a virginal conception is rare and obviously an adaptation of existing myths. For example, Plato was said to have been fathered by Apollo, and both Alexander the Great and Heracles by Zeus. In some sources, the conceptions of Plato and Alexander are said to be virginal.

mother who denies that Joseph (or anyone else) is the father? Might her protestations just be a cover-up for her loose living?' How credible, they might wonder, can be the claim of Jesus to have such an important place in God's work, if he had (in their eyes) an uncertain pedigree?

In addition, as undoubtedly a *single* mother conceived Jesus, those who disbelieved the claims about the virginal conception might well also add that Jesus' mother *must have* contravened the Old Testament law of God, as she was pregnant when unmarried. This objection highlights two difficulties.

The first difficulty is that since Mary had broken the law, it was *impossible* for God to have chosen her to be the mother of the saviour. The reasoning would be as follows. The penalty for being an unmarried pregnant woman was death by stoning. The child could not be the saviour, because, if God's laws had been properly followed, Mary would have been executed, and the pregnancy would not have gone to full term and the child delivered alive.

The second difficulty is that to claim that God sent his son to be carried in the womb of an unmarried woman is, in effect, to claim that God had played 'fast and loose' with his own moral standards. The law was clear: sexual relations and procreation were for marriage and for marriage alone. God would not require Mary to have sexual relations before marriage. To claim otherwise is, in effect, to say that God is capricious.[3] To borrow Paul's idea from a different context,[4] if God required Mary to be an unmarried mother, God would be promoting sinful behaviour. (Paul vigorously denies that God would do this.) Just as the first objection insists that God *would* not have allowed the saviour to be born to an unmarried mother, so this objection insists that God *could* not do this.

The result of these concerns about Jesus' origins was to undermine Jesus' claims to be the one who fulfilled God's messianic purposes.[5] Many regarded him as no more than a local boy, the son of Joseph whose wife had conceived him before marriage by the agency of a man. They also thought that his family was nothing out of the ordinary.[6]

A third way that we see the humility of God is in the timing and place of Jesus' birth.

Jesus was born in a Roman province near the outer edge of the Roman Empire. Jesus lived in Nazareth, a village in the north of Palestine, in an area known as 'Galilee'. In that area, literacy was limited and what was important was more often remembered

---

[3]Paul vigorously refutes the idea that God could compromise his own integrity and be the agent of sin in Romans 9 and 11, in a discussion about a different subject.
[4]Romans 6.1, 15.
[5]See Luke 4.21.
[6]Luke 4.22 and Matthew 13.55–56.

than written down. Galilee was known for its characteristic regional accent.[7] It was some distance from Jerusalem, the centre of Jewish learning and worship. In addition, those to whom Jesus spoke were usually farmers and peasants, artisans, children and women. They were not the 'movers and shakers' of the Roman world whose approval would have ensured that Jesus and what he did would have been taken seriously and widely discussed.

Even if reports about Jesus were known about outside Palestine, one can well imagine a Roman saying, 'Who really values or believes what people there say anyway? After all, they are no more than simple, uneducated peasants.' (Nathaniel, who was himself from Palestine, said much the same of Jesus in John 1.46.) That Jesus did not write books, have a formal Greek education or speak to influential Romans in public places meant, in the eyes of some, that what he taught *could* not be well founded, credible or persuasive. At best, his teachings were the thoughts of a country boy, of passing interest only.

These factors amount to a significant risk that only a generation or two of people in an obscure part of the Roman Empire would have remembered Jesus' teachings, miracles, death and resurrection.

The magnitude of God's humility is, therefore, disclosed through the risks Jesus faced in being born as a human being,

---

[7] See Matthew 26.73.

through what seemed to be scandalous claims about Jesus' conception and parenthood, and through the relative obscurity of Jesus' life and ministry.

Jesus, of course, *lived with* the humility of God. He faced temptation, just like any other human being, and he had no greater resources than you or I to resist that temptation.[8] He faced choices about whether to believe or disbelieve God, to obey or disobey God and whether to be selfish (and live for himself) or to live in surrender to God's will.

Jesus also *practised* the humility of God in the way he lived. He did not bully people to make them do what he wanted. As Paul wrote in a different context, Jesus appeals to humanity through the apostles to respond to his love and grace and urges people not to disparage the gifts of God's grace.[9] He does not constrain them to believe. Jesus said to those who were arresting him at Gethsemane that God could have sent 'more than 12 legions of angels' to protect and rescue him.[10] (There could be up to 6,000 men in a fully staffed legion, and so Jesus here is referring to a possible 72,000 angels protecting him.) Instead of resisting, he yielded to a barbarous death.

Jesus' life, therefore, from conception to death and all that lies in between, point us to the humility of God, and so reveal

---

[8]Matthew 4.1–11.
[9]2 Corinthians 5.20 and 6.1.
[10]Matthew 26.53.

the character of God. Jesus did this more fully, more profoundly and more extensively than anyone before or since. He is the lens by which we see and understand God's humility with unique clarity.

There is one thing more to say to complete this reflection on the humility of God.

In describing Jesus' God-like humility and surrender to death in Philippians 2.5–8, Paul says in the following verse that *therefore* God exalted Jesus and restored him to his proper identity and place.

It is as if there is an inescapable law of causality in the universe: those who live in humility, with all the vulnerability and risk that go with living that way, can be sure that God will vindicate them in God's way and at God's appointed time. It is not that we live in a meaningless universe, in which chance rules. Inbuilt into the pattern of the universe is God's immutable law that God will vindicate and honour those who live reflecting and practising his humility.

We do not need, therefore, to be fearful of practising the virtue of humility, despite the way so many today disparage it. Those who have the courage to practise it will receive grace and, in God's time, honour and reward.[11]

---

[11] 1 Peter 5.5–6.

Christmas . . . and shepherds

The shepherds returned, glorifying and praising
God that everything they had heard and seen
was as they had been told.

LUKE 2.20

Picture the scene.

Near Bethlehem, a group of shepherds was looking after their sheep one night.

The shepherds would know each one of their sheep.

Perhaps to those of us who live in towns, one sheep looks and sounds very much like another; but this is not the case. Sheep have individual cries and look distinctive, just like any other animal when you get to know it. A good shepherd would be able to recognize each of the sheep; the sheep in a flock would know and recognize their shepherd.[1] The shepherds in Luke 2 would have been no different.

Sheep were easy prey for wild animals and for thieves.[2] It was necessary, especially at night, to ensure the sheep were safe from harm.

So on this day, after dark (and as they usually did), the shepherds put the sheep in a walled enclosure. The enclosure was probably made of stone or out of tightly matted bushes. At least one of the shepherds lay across the opening, to stop unwelcome visitors from entering and to make sure that none of the sheep wandered off into danger. The shepherd may even have been asleep, as he lay across the opening.

We are familiar with the rest of the story, especially because of the popularity of Nahum Tate's carol, 'While Shepherds Watched Their Flocks by Night'.[3] An angel came and told the shepherds that in Bethlehem a saviour had recently been born. The shepherds were frightened. The angel told the shepherds how to identify the newborn saviour:[4] he would be wrapped in strips of cloth (not unusual) and would be lying in a cattle trough (very unusual). The shepherds then went and found the child. In due course, after speaking to Mary and Joseph and

---

[1]John 10.3, 5.

[2]For example, John 10.1.

[3]When we lived in Yorkshire, we sang the carol to the tune *On Ilkley Moor Bar T'at*.

[4]Luke 2.12.

to others about what the angels had told them, the shepherds returned to the hills of Bethlehem and to the sheep.

What we should note is a point that is often missed: the shepherds (or, at least, most of them) left their normally well-cared sheep unguarded. Anyone could have come to steal the sheep. A wild animal could have harried or killed them. The sheep could have wandered off in different directions, far from the pen.

To leave sheep in this way is very unusual behaviour for shepherds, and highlights the fact that what the angels had said to the shepherds caused them to do something exceptional and even (so some might say) foolish.

We should also note that the shepherds were, as it were, 'minding their own business', going about their ordinary work with the sheep. Then an angel appeared, and both terrified and thrilled them.

Several implications arise from these simple observations about the story.

The first is that something happened to the shepherds that was so astonishingly important and life-changing that in response, they left their sheep. The sheep *were* important and their safety *did* matter. However, in view of what the angel said and of the instructions the angel left, it became *more* important and *more* pressing for the shepherds to respond to what the angel told them to do.

Sometimes, God comes into our lives and causes us to rethink or redirect what we are doing. This may mean we make dramatic changes to our lives, such as we see later in the Gospels with Simon Peter, Andrew, James and John.[5]

For most of us, the changes may often apparently be more modest: for example, we may decide to end a relationship or a habit, or to begin to do something new.

However, *whatever* we do is significant, whether it feels that way to us or not, because the changes are *our* response to *God's* work in our lives. We do the equivalent of leaving sheep – and we need to trust that, by responding to God's call and following him, we are doing what is right, even if we have doubts about that at the time.

The second implication is that sometimes God's call may come to us when we least expect it or when we may not want it. C. S. Lewis famously was 'surprised' to find that he was called into faith, and thought himself to be one of the unlikeliest new followers of Jesus in England.[6] His experience, though, is not unusual, and some find that God draws them to himself at times and in ways they did not expect. Almost certainly, the shepherds would not have guessed in the hours before the angel came to them that they were shortly to have an encounter that would change their lives forever.

---

[5] Mark 1.16–20.
[6] *Surprised by Joy: An Account of My Early Life* (London: Geoffrey Bles, 1955).

God's call can sometimes come dramatically and unexpect-
edly, as it did to the shepherds, or it may be the result of devel-
oping awareness, over a long period. It is important that we
hold ourselves ready to respond to God's call in whichever way
it may come to us.[7]

If we read the story of the shepherds thoughtfully, we
may also be left wondering why God came to *shepherds*
(who in consequence had to leave their sheep unattended)
and not, for example, to a Levite or a Pharisee or someone
at home at leisure? Such people could have gone to visit the
newborn child, probably without neglecting an important
responsibility.

The reasons are simple.

First, God does not always speak first to the wise, the well
educated and those who are sophisticated. Sometimes, as here,
he comes to people who might be called simple, with little education, who show just as much understanding – sometimes
perhaps even more – as people who are better educated and
have had better opportunities and more advantages. Despite
the shepherds' apparent lack of privileges, they understood
the significance of what the angels said, and responded wisely,
instinctively and immediately. As Paul says in a different context in 1 Corinthians 1.26–31, God sometimes chooses *first* the

---

[7] See Luke 9.57–62 and 14.16–24.

'also-rans' – those who are despised or undervalued – and not clever or well-qualified people.[8]

Secondly, in the Old Testament, God is often depicted as being like a shepherd, caring for and nurturing his people. This metaphor points us to God's loyalty, devotion and protective care. The Old Testament also depicts good leaders as being like shepherds, for though God was the principal shepherd (leader) of the people, responsible and loving under-shepherds were also needed, to give the people a visible shepherd.[9] Writers in the New Testament sometimes refer to Jesus as a 'shepherd' or as the 'good shepherd'.[10] The fact that Jesus was born in Bethlehem, the place of origin of David, one of Israel's most famous shepherds who later became a great leader, subtly connects the birth of a 'saviour, the anointed Lord'[11] with David, an illustrious forebear from whom Jesus was descended and whose life and example he would greatly surpass.

The shepherds went to visit (and presumably, to worship) the saviour who had been born on earth. He was, indeed, 'great David's greater son' (in the words of James Montgomery's hymn, 'Hail to the Lord's anointed') who had come not only as leader but also as loving shepherd, to save his people from

---

[8]We explored this theme in more detail on 6 December.

[9]Numbers 27.1. See Matthew 9.36.

[10]See, for example, John 10.1–18, 22–29 and 1 Peter 2.25 and 5.4.

[11]Luke 2.11.

their sins and, in watchful love, to protect them for eternity. The shepherds went to see the greater shepherd for whom Israel had longed for more than a millennium and who had now been born.

Today, God calls all those with responsibility in Christian communities to act as if they were shepherds, nurturing those with whom they have been entrusted.

Some of us may hold 'major' roles, with the care and oversight of many people. Others of us may have what we regard as a modest responsibility in a local community of believers. (This may include, for example, stewarding people to their seats for public worship or serving refreshments afterwards.)

Whatever God calls us to do, we are all to exercise an equal measure of loving, caring oversight of those we encounter. Like the shepherds, we thereby serve 'the shepherd and guardian of our souls', Jesus Christ.[12] The result will be that we properly fulfil our task of being under-shepherds of God's flock.

---

[12] 1 Peter 2.25.

DECEMBER 17

Christmas . . . and Anna

Anna . . . did not leave the Temple. Night and day,
she worshipped with fasting and prayers

LUKE 2.37

One of the neglected people in the Christmas accounts is Anna.[1] There are some important principles in the 59 words that Luke devotes to her.

First, Anna had 'lived for very long'.[2] Quite how long is hard to work out from what Luke wrote. She may have been 84 years old in total or she may have been widowed for 84 years.[3] It is

---

[1]Luke 2.36–38.

[2]Luke 2.36.

[3]We also learn from Luke that Anna lived with her husband 'seven years from her virginity'. This is a difficult phrase to understand, and probably means that she was engaged for seven years in total. The point Luke seems to be making is that Anna was a woman of self-discipline and self-control, as she did not consummate

not clear which is the case from Luke's words, though most English translations suggest Luke meant to say that she was 84 years old. If we take Luke's words as meaning that she was widowed for 84 years, then it is likely that Anna was more than 100 years old.[4]

When we think of people aged 84, what comes to our minds? Vibrant, active members of the Church? Leaders in the community? Perhaps, for some nearer to 84 years than in excess of 100 years. Even so, we can sometimes be patronizing and condescending about such people, saying that he or she 'is not bad for their age, considering'. ('Considering what?', I sometimes wonder.)

Anna *was* vibrant and active in her faith and she sounds a remarkable person for *any* age. She was a 'prophetess', one of the few women prophetesses in the period before Jesus. Only Miriam, Deborah, Huldah, Noadiah and Isaiah's unnamed wife are called 'prophetesses'.[5]

Anna does not fit the stereotype of an older person. She seems to have spent most of her time in the Temple, active in worship. Luke tells us she fasted regularly and prayed much, both in the day and at night. God seems to have been her focus

---

her marriage for seven years. See the reflection headed 11 December on the two stages to marriage in the era of Jesus.

[4]The sums are not difficult to do: at the earliest, Anna would have been engaged at age 12 and so married at age 19, after a seven-year engagement. This would then make her at least one hundred and three years old.

[5]Exodus 15.20, Judges 4.4, 2 Kings 22.14, Nehemiah 6.14 and Isaiah 8.3. Noadiah is called a 'false' prophetess.

and delight, and her life seems to be characterized by a deep spirituality and passion for God.

Anna met Jesus in the Temple in the following way.

In Jewish thought, contact with blood made a person ritually unclean. To be ritually unclean did not mean that one was dirty and so needed to wash. Rather, it meant that one was not allowed to enter the Temple or to touch things that were regarded as holy. For obvious reasons, giving birth rendered a person 'ritually unclean'. It was, therefore, necessary for Mary to present herself in the Temple to offer a sacrifice to mark the end of the period of her 'uncleanness'. Leviticus 12.1–8 laid down that in the case of a male child, the offering should be 40 days after his birth.

Anna was in the Temple when Mary's time for 'purification' came. When Anna saw Jesus in the Temple with Mary and Joseph, she had a prophetic revelation about who Jesus was and began to praise God that the long-awaited Messiah had been born. In her excitement and enthusiasm about whom she had seen, she spoke about Jesus to 'all' who were eagerly expecting the coming of the Messiah and the redemptive work that he would do.

The Temple would have been teeming with people when Mary and Joseph entered with Jesus, and I expect they would have been among hundreds of other people who were praying, worshipping and making sacrifices. There was nothing to mark them out as special or different. Yet Anna, through the prophetic revelation, identified Jesus as the Messiah and was unafraid to speak about Jesus to all who were longing that the Messiah should come.

Anna challenges our preconceptions about what it means to be 'old'.

First, she clearly did not think she had completed her life's work. Rather, to the extent that was appropriate for her age, she was vigorous, active and thinking about the future. She may well have guessed that she would not live to see the work of the Messiah whom she saw as a 6-week-old child. That did not stop her from rejoicing at his birth and speaking about him to those who were longing for the Messiah to come.

Being active for God does not end when our youth or young adulthood have passed. It may be true that younger people have more energy and often more by way of ideals than we who may be older and less physically fit. That does not mean that we cannot serve God and focus on living for him. It also does not mean that God will not use us. God gave Anna insight about the significance of a newborn child, and she had the courage to speak about that child to all who shared her longing for the Messiah to come.

Another preconception that Anna challenges is that elderly people are not typically enthusiastic about God or enthusiastic for God. In contrast to what we sometimes assume, perhaps patronizingly, about older people, Anna was vibrant in her faith. She worshipped, she fasted and she prayed, and not just one day a week and not just for short periods each day. Rather, night and day she was in the Temple, actively engaging with God.

Lastly, in the twenty-first century, many people of Anna's age feel 'useless' and undervalued. In contrast, Anna clearly believed God could still use her, and she made sure she was available for God to use her if he wished. In Anna's mind, it was not a case of privileges and revelations only for the young. The result was the prophetic revelation she received about Jesus and opportunities to speak about Jesus to people who were longing for the coming of the Messiah into the world.

Her example presents a challenge to us. In senior years, it is perhaps too easy to choose to enjoy the comfort of the television and the armchair, thinking that our opportunities for service and for worship are dimmed or diminished. Not so at all. In Anna's case, a lifetime of piety and devotion was continuing to deepen in old age. She did not stay at home, thinking she deserved a well-earned rest. Instead, she was in the Temple, the centre of worship and activity, and so came across Mary, Joseph and Jesus.

We are in danger of undervaluing the elderly among us. We are also in danger of assuming that those who are senior in years are of diminished value to the Church and (dare we say it?) to God. Rather, the maturity that comes from a lifetime of worship and faith makes such people finely honed tools in the hands of God to teach us who are younger and less experienced. The challenge to the Church is how to encourage, foster and develop all people, including its senior members.

Those of us who are younger would be wise to ask ourselves how we might promote the ministries of those who are of senior years among us. We neglect the maturity and experience of our senior members to our loss and to the loss of the wider Church.

DECEMBER 18

Christmas . . . and Simeon

Simeon took Jesus in his arms and praised God. He said,
'Lord, now you are letting your servant leave in peace,
as you have said you would'.

LUKE 2.28

We think that the birth of Jesus is about beginnings, as indeed it is. For some people, however, it was about endings.

Luke tells us about Simeon, who had waited patiently for the coming of the Messiah.[1] God had told him that he would not die until he had seen the Messiah. Once Simeon had witnessed Jesus' coming he was able to give thanks to God. Simeon said he could go away, settled and at peace, since what Israel had longed for was at last happening.[2]

---

[1]Luke 2.25.
[2]Luke 2.29.

We assume that Simeon was an old man and that he was saying he could die in peace. There is nothing in the text of the Gospel of Luke that says this. You will see, if you read Luke 2.25–35 carefully, that Simeon says only that he could leave, at peace with himself, knowing that the Messiah had come.

It does not matter for our purposes whether Simeon was young or old. What matters is that he knew the waiting was over. For him, an ending had occurred (the waiting for the Messiah to be born) and that he was ready to move on (presumably, to experience the blessings the Messiah would bring).

Endings are important, as any psychotherapist will tell us. An end places a divider between what has been and what is to come. Ending well is important for moving forward in life (or even into death) in the right frame of mind.

I once worked with a man who had a somewhat unhappy relationship with his wife. (I will call them 'Brian' and 'Julia' in this context.) One day Brian and Julia were going to the cinema, and they were late and at risk of missing the start of the film. On the way, they had a disagreement about whether Brian should stop at a set of traffic lights, or whether he should 'jump' them by driving across on amber. Brian ignored what Julia wanted, and did not drive across on the amber light. When the lights turned green again, he continued the journey. Very shortly after, the driver of another car drove into Brian's car at high speed, killing Julia instantly.

Brian was left with the thought that if he had done as Julia had asked and not stopped at the traffic lights, Julia would not have been killed. He also knew that their last conversation had been an unresolved disagreement.

I saw Brian in my clinic because he was suffering from psychological trauma. This was not only because of the accident but also because he had not finished well with Julia.

Brian was not to blame that he and Julia had not managed to make their peace with one another before her premature death. Only seconds had elapsed between their disagreement and the accident. Even so, he was left with a feeling of 'unfinished business'.

We do not know when we will die or when someone we know will die. In view of this, the writer of Ephesians 4.26 is wise to say that we should not let the sun go down on our anger. It is important to live in a state of being ready to finish our lives and to keep seeking to finish our business as we go through life, and not just when we anticipate that death might be near.

Letting go, admitting that an ending is coming, and moving on, can be immensely challenging when a loved one moves from illness into terminal illness. It is important for us and for those we love that we acknowledge when death is approaching, and to prepare ourselves (and those we love) for this usually very unwelcome event.

I had a friend ('Susan') whose elderly husband was evidently dying, and it was a very painful ending. Susan tried to convince her husband that he would 'get better soon', thereby not allowing herself or her husband to prepare for what was inevitable. I am not suggesting that she should have given up hope; what I am saying is that it is helpful to have sufficient courage to accept what is almost certainly to come.

Anyone who has spent time with a dying person who has a clear faith will probably be able to affirm this. It can be immensely uplifting when someone with faith plans their affairs well, including the details of his or her funeral. I recall a very uplifting funeral I once attended, where the deceased had 'finished her business', as had her family with her. Her funeral felt like a true celebration of her life, an ending of something that had been a gift to many.

Of course, endings do not come only when a life ends, as is perhaps the case with Simeon. It is important, for example, to place an ending on anything that marks a time of significant change. When people leave one job for another, they generally celebrate leaving their job with the event marked in some way. Young people generally celebrate the ending of childhood and the start of adulthood, although the age for this celebration differs between cultures and communities. Marriage can mark the end of singlehood and the start of being a couple, although in communities where people live together for long periods before marriage this divider becomes blurred. Divorce can also mark an important ending, and signal the start of something new, even if the ending signals that all did not progress in a way that met hopes and expectations.

Marking these changes is an important 'rite of passage', and is helpful to sustain good mental health. It helps to close the end of one era of our lives and to start a new one. We might be frightened to acknowledge that there is an ending because we fear the change that a new beginning will bring: but if we do not acknowledge the ending, we will not properly move on.

When I was studying for my doctoral degree, I met many people who had found it hard to complete their doctoral dissertations. One friend struggled on for 20 years!

Most people finished their doctorates, but a number did not. Some eventually gave up and moved on to something else. In an odd way, I always quietly admired these people. It struck me as requiring a great deal *more* courage to mark an end by admitting defeat and then to move onto something new. It is better to do that than to struggle on, making little or no progress over a long period of time. Without an admission of defeat and an ending, it would have been very difficult for these people to move on to something else in a psychologically healthy way. It can be very important to admit when something is just not going the way we would like it to, and to move on.

Related to this, I recall someone I knew ('Emily') who felt that she had been badly treated by her employer. Her working conditions had changed; she had not felt able to agree to the new conditions and therefore resigned from her job. Emily felt that she was entitled to some compensation. She tried every avenue available, including seeking legal advice and an independent review. The advice did not go the way she would have liked it to. Emily felt unable to give up, to put an ending on the matter, and to move on. Her mental health deteriorated and she became seriously depressed. As a result, her marriage ended. She became unable to work at all and to pursue any of the things that had given her enjoyment previously.

As an onlooker, I was somewhat baffled that *anything* to do with a job could be so valuable as to affect the quality of her life so dramatically and so damagingly. Emily evidently disagreed. She was unable to recognize and accept the end of her job, signalling a time to move on. She did not give herself permission to look ahead and see what else life might have offered, albeit in a form that she had not expected.

Endings come in many different ways in our lives. Simeon marked the ending of his period of waiting to see the Messiah by taking Jesus in his arms and blessing him and his parents. He knew that in the ending there was also a new beginning, the next stage of the fulfilment of the messianic promises.

Are there endings that you have avoided facing? How can you now acknowledge and face them? How can you mark the endings, even if to do so will be painful? In marking the endings, which new beginnings do you face?

The new beginnings may be hard to identify at first, but there is *always* a beginning after an ending. How we end will shape how we negotiate the new beginning.

DECEMBER 19

Christmas . . . and the Magi

Magi came from the east to Jerusalem.

MATTHEW 2.1

You will be disappointed, as you read this reflection, if you are sure there were three wise men and that they were kings called Caspar, Melchior and Balthazar.

Who were the people that we usually call 'the three kings'?

Matthew 2.1 says *magoi* (from which we get 'Magi') came to Jerusalem. The Magi said that they had read in the stars about the birth of the king of the Jews and they wanted to know where he was to be born.

We know from elsewhere that Magi were Zoroastrian scholars or priests from the modern-day area of Iran, who would have been, according to various ancient writers, experts in astrology, the interpretation of dreams and perhaps alchemy.

The truth is that we cannot infer very much more about the Magi. They are mysterious, shadowy figures and, despite the way many carols and Christmas cards celebrate them, we know very little about them.

Matthew does not tell us how many Magi there were or what their names were. Popular tradition has it that there were three Magi because they presented three gifts to Jesus out of their treasure chests. The presentation of the gifts is supposed to be the origin of the practice of giving Christmas presents. (Did the Magi realize what they were starting?) Popular tradition also has it that the Magi were 'wise' and 'kings', but that is not how Matthew describes them. People also assume that the Magi were men; they probably were, but not necessarily. So the three wise men who were kings and who are sung about so often may not have numbered three, were not called 'wise' or 'kings' and were only probably, but not necessarily, men. (Even so, singing 'We three kings of Orient are' is, nevertheless, part of a 'traditional Christmas' for some people.)

Another popular myth – reflected in the calendar of many churches – is that the Magi came to Jesus 12 days after he was born. This cannot be so because shortly after the visit of the Magi, Jesus and his family fled to Egypt, where they remained for several months until Herod's death. We have seen that Jesus and his family were in the Temple in Jerusalem 40 days after

Jesus' birth. They would not have been able to go to the Temple if they were already in exile in Egypt.[1]

Despite the fact that we know relatively little about the Magi, there are, however, at least four important observations that we can make about the Magi who visited Jesus.

First, the Magi were clearly astrologers. They had observed a star that they had interpreted as meaning a child had been born who would be king of the Jews.

Secondly, the Magi also knew how to interpret dreams because they properly interpreted a dream as meaning they were not to go back from Bethlehem to Herod's Jerusalem but to return home by a different route.

Next, they seem to have been people of wealth because they brought costly gifts for Jesus and had the resources to travel a long way.

Lastly, we can infer that the Magi were Gentiles, not Jews.

The fact that the Magi were astrologers and Gentiles is significant.

Magic and astrology get a bad press in the Bible but not when it comes to the Magi. The odd thing is that, though the Magi practised arts that were forbidden in the Old Testament and

---

[1]Matthew 2.1–8 does *not* imply that Jesus was newborn, only that he was still a baby. We can infer that Mary and Joseph stayed in Bethlehem for some time after Jesus was born, probably as 'migrant workers' (to use today's terminology).

clearly frowned upon in other contexts in the New Testament,[2] they are not the subject of any criticism in Matthew 2. If anything, Matthew treats the Magi with admiration and respect: they came to seek and pay homage to Jesus. Neither did they fall for Herod's ruse to use them to identify, and so murder, the future king of Israel.

Matthew is, I think, pointing us to something significant about the birth of Jesus. Not only did the Jewish Scriptures clearly say where the saviour-king was to be born[3] but also other sources of learning, outside the world of Jewish thought and practice, were pointing to the birth of Jesus. Here was no ordinary child. Here was a child who held a special place in the purposes of God for *all* people. Those who pursued truth and knowledge, whether from studying the prophecies of the Jewish Scriptures or from observing the natural order (even through astrological arts), could rightly discern something about the significant events that were happening at the time.

Importantly, no one tradition disclosed all that there was to know: the Scriptures disclosed where the saviour-king was to be born, but not when; the Magi knew that he had been born, but not where. What God was revealing in disparate places had to be brought together for the full picture.

---

[2]See Acts 8.9–13 and 13.6–11.
[3]Matthew 2.5, 6.

For us today, this points to the integrity of seeking to know more about the natural order, through scientific and other endeavour. What has been created points to its creator.[4] As we study what is in the world and learn from the findings of people in other (that is, non-theological) disciplines who also study what is in the world, we will discover more of the creator God. Scripture has its place in interpreting these data and, importantly but sometimes not properly recognized, these data have *their* place in interpreting Scripture.

I said it was also significant that the Magi were Gentiles, that is, they were not Jewish. As Gentiles, they came to pay homage to 'the child who has been born *king of the Jews*'.[5] They did not say that they had come to pay homage to 'the child who has been born *saviour of the world*'.

What Matthew wants us to realize is that the Magi came to seek out someone they believed to be an important figure for the *Jewish* people, and as Gentiles, they came to pay homage to that child. Perhaps uncomfortably for us today, Matthew is emphasizing the priority of the Jews in the plan and purposes of God at this time, and the subordinate position of the Gentiles.

Even so, Gentiles were not excluded from paying homage to Jesus. Although Jesus was to be 'the king of the *Jews*', the

---

[4] Romans 1.20.
[5] Matthew 2.2.

Magi clearly believed from their astrological observations that he was of more widespread significance. They sensed that Jesus would have some sort of call on all peoples in the world. They also believed that it was appropriate for them to pay homage to (or 'to worship') Jesus. For these reasons, they came with their gifts for Jesus.

The Gospel of Matthew goes on to make clear that Gentiles will be fully integrated into and share in what God purposes for the world through the child that the Magi sought out, and this would be on an equal footing with the Jews. For example, early on in the Gospel, in one of Jesus' first healings,[6] Jesus heals a centurion's servant. He was the Gentile servant of a Gentile Roman soldier. Jesus then says that people from all parts of the world (that is, both Jews *and* Gentiles) will come and worship God in the kingdom of heaven. Jesus adds that Jews who disbelieve will be excluded.[7] All who worship God through Jesus will do so on an equal footing: by faith and not through genetic or racial privileges.[8]

To end any doubt, if any remained, Jesus' last words in the Gospel of Matthew are that the disciples are to take the gospel to 'all nations'. Significantly for Matthew's listeners and readers, the word for 'nations' can also be translated 'Gentiles'. In other

---

[6]Matthew 8.5–13.
[7]Matthew 8.12.
[8]Matthew 8.10–11.

words, the gospel is for all people, Jew and Gentile alike, and the king of the Jews, to whom the Magi came to pay homage, is the king of all people and of all creation.

The Magi brought gifts in homage to Jesus. What can we do in response?

Despite the sentimentality of some of the earlier verses of Christina Rossetti's 'In the Bleak Midwinter', the last verse beautifully expresses an appropriate response to 'the child who has been born king of the Jews'. The greatest we can give God is ourselves, expressed in the carol as our 'hearts'.

Christmas . . . and presents

When the Magi entered the house, they saw the baby with his mother, Mary. They prostrated themselves before him and paid him homage. Then they opened their treasure chests and presented him with gifts of gold, frankincense and myrrh.

MATTHEW 2.11

What did Mary and Joseph do with the gold, frankincense and myrrh that the Magi brought Jesus?

I suspect that whatever eventually happened to the gifts, the gifts must have been at least a little *unwelcome*. This is because of what the gifts would have meant to thinking people at the time, and because of what they would certainly have meant to Mary and Joseph.

The simplest interpretation of what the gifts mean is that they are tokens of homage and worship. They indicate something about the worth and significance of the person to whom they were being given. By the gifts, the Magi were indicating that Jesus was no ordinary baby but someone who was worthy to receive costly gifts (brought in treasure chests) that they carried from a far-off country. The Magi even prostrated themselves as they gave the child the gifts. (Perhaps here there is a foretaste of what John says in Revelation 4.11 about Jesus after he had completed his work on earth. John writes that Jesus was 'worthy . . . to receive power and wealth, wisdom and might, honour, glory and praise'.) Despite the worship and the generous gifts, these gifts were, for the reasons we shall explore later, almost certainly unwelcome.

This interpretation is perhaps a little too simple, as the gifts (gold, frankincense and myrrh) were clearly intended to symbolize something about the child whom the Magi were visiting. The gifts were perhaps intended to point to his identity, role and significance.

The traditional interpretation, explored and developed by the early Church Fathers such as Irenaeus (AD 130–202), Clement of Alexandria (AD 150–211/216) and Origen (AD 185–254), for example, is that the gifts do tell us something specific about who Jesus is and what the future held for him.

The gold, so these early Church Fathers suggest, points to Jesus as king. Not as king in a secular sense, ruling over a portion of land, raising an army, levying taxes and enforcing laws.

He was king in the sense that God had entrusted to him 'all authority in heaven and on earth' following the events of Good Friday and Easter Sunday.[1] There would come a day when all people would recognize that Jesus was more than a Jewish religious activist who fell foul of the Romans. Rather, people would acknowledge him for who he truly was. He was God's son and the one who, at the end of time, would right the world's wrongs and be worshipped, as saviour and redeemer of all things, in a new heaven and a new earth.[2]

The frankincense, secondly, alludes to Jesus as God. The little baby whom the Magi worshipped was not only a human being. Christian traditions in their developed form teach that he was also God. Jesus' two identities (if 'identities' is the right word) – human and divine – coexisted, so the early Church Fathers concluded, in his one body.[3]

In Jesus' lifetime, I suspect people had little difficulty believing that he was a human being, as indeed he truly was. He ate, he drank, he slept, as we all do. Like us, he had to wash. He, too, suffered from physical ailments. As a baby, he probably wore what we now call 'nappies' (or 'diapers') and had to be toilet trained. He was educated and taught to read and write, to spell and to reason. Like all children, he would have scraped

---

[1] Matthew 28.18.
[2] Revelation 20.11–21.5.
[3] We think further about this on 24 December.

his knees and probably had childhood nightmares. His parents would have comforted him. (I doubt that 'Away in a Manger' is right to suggest that Jesus did not cry as a child!) Like us, he learned about God, about faith and about his role through the Scriptures. For all its sentimentality, Jesus' humanity is what the third verse of Mrs C. F. Alexander's carol 'Once in Royal David's city' rightly powerfully portrays. The difficulty that people had in Jesus' day, as some people still have today, is to believe that Jesus was more than a human being, even a very good human being, who had profound insights about people and new interpretations of traditional orthodoxies.

The traditions of the Church teach us that Jesus is more than a human being. Certainly, the New Testament writers see Jesus as someone who supremely and uniquely reveals the God in whom the Jews believed. He is also calling all people to believe both in God and in himself as God's son. J. D. G. Dunn adds: '. . . for the first Christians Jesus was seen to be not only the one by whom believers come to God, but also the one by whom God has come to believers'.[4]

The Nicene Creed (adopted by 'the First Ecumenical Council' that met at Nicaea in AD 325) and the later Athanasian Creed (probably originating in the late fifth-century or early

---

[4]*Did the First Christians Worship Jesus? The New Testament Evidence* (London: SPCK, 2010), p. 151.

sixth-century AD)[5] spell out the later conclusions of the Church Fathers. You can find these words in, for example, the *Book of Common Prayer* (1662) and *Common Worship* (2000), both used by the Church of England in services.[6] Charles Wesley captured something of the theology of the creeds in the carol, 'Let earth and heaven combine'. In the carol, he writes of 'the incarnate deity' who is 'our God, contracted to a span, incomprehensibly made man'.

Lastly, myrrh looks to Jesus' death, for myrrh was a perfume used to embalm bodies. After Jesus died and had been taken down from the cross, Nicodemus brought a large quantity of myrrh and aloes to embalm Jesus' body.[7] He and Joseph of Arimathea, in accordance with Jewish customs, wrapped Jesus' body, with the spices, in strips of linen cloth.

Why myrrh with the gold and frankincense? Why point to Jesus' death at the same time as pointing to his kingship and divinity?

The reason is that all three are interconnected and one cannot have any one without both of the others. He who is the son of God and the exalted king of all also yielded to the cross as a human being. Even at his birth, the cross is prefigured as

---

[5]The Athanasian Creed is sometimes known as 'Quicunque Vult' from the Latin words at the start of the Creed.

[6]The version of the Nicene Creed used in *Common Worship* is based on the version agreed at the English Language Liturgical Consultation (1988).

[7]John 19.38–40.

integral to who Jesus is and the exalted place he later held. The gold of Jesus' exalted kingship, the frankincense of Jesus as son of God and the myrrh of his death on the cross *together* now touch and benefit every human being who looks to God in faith. Christmas, Good Friday and Easter Sunday are indissolubly linked.

So why might these gifts have been unwelcome to Mary and Joseph? What was it about them that would have made them unsettling?

Quite simply, because the gifts probably *intruded*.

If we are honest, we long that our children be happy, settled and safe when they are adults. Maybe we hope our children will marry and have children, that they will have successful careers and that they will be held in high esteem in their communities. (We thought about this in the reflection headed 9 December when we thought about what Elizabeth and Zechariah may have hoped for their son, John.)

The gifts the Magi gave Jesus pointed to something different for Jesus. They pointed to a role, to a plan and to a purpose laid out by God for Jesus that in their entirety would *not* have been many parents' hope for a child. The unique circumstances of Jesus' conception, the strange visitors following his birth and the prophecies about Jesus would have left Joseph and Mary in no doubt that their child was no ordinary child and that his life, and their lives too, almost certainly would have pain and suffering in consequence.[8] The Magi's gifts reinforced what Jesus' parents probably already knew: that Jesus, though Messiah, would live a life marred by suffering and conflict and that they too would face a measure of suffering because of their son.

Sometimes there are intrusions in our lives that tell us about or remind us of things we do not want to know or face. Perhaps an illness that points to advancing years. Maybe a letter or phone call that reminds us of something we are ashamed of from the past. Perhaps it is a piece of music that reminds us of former unhappiness or an event that dissipates our hopes for the future. It might even be circumstances moving us in a direction – such as towards a new role, career or ministry – that we ourselves would not have chosen.

Though these intrusions may be unwelcome and painful, God is present in the intrusions. When Paul listed human disaster and misery, he also reminded his readers that nothing could separate them from God's love and from knowing God's help and vindication.[9] What intrudes may not be what we want or what we had hoped for; it may even be crushing and heartbreaking. It does not mean that God has abandoned us.

At a point of deep despair when, in the sixth-century BC, the Jewish people had been sent into exile and their hopes and confidence broken, God said to Jeremiah and the exiled Israelites,

---

[8]For example, Simeon later foretold in prophetic words that Mary would face anguish as sharp as a sword piercing her body (Luke 2.35).
[9]Romans 8.35–39.

'I know the plans I have for you. They are plans for your welfare and not for evil. They give you a future and hope.'[10]

In varying degrees, we all face, from time to time, what is (at least) unwelcome in our lives or (at worst) what we fear will destroy our hope and confidence.

God does not abandon us at such times, even though we may feel that he has. 'There is no pit so deep that God's love in not deeper still', said Betsy ten Boom to her sister Corrie, shortly before Betsy died in Ravensbrück concentration camp in 1944.[11]

In our difficulties, God sometimes reaches out to us, so that we can take hold of and feel his love. At other times, we cling on by faith to the knowledge that God loves us, even though it does not feel or seem that way. Our apparent solitude and isolation are not because God has abandoned us but because God wants us to walk not by sight (or by feelings) but by faith.[12] Jesus himself knew that isolation on the cross;[13] we should not be surprised if we too sometimes experience it.

Whatever we may experience, it is important that we look, not to what we see and feel (because these are temporary) but to God and to what is eternal.[14] The unwelcome gifts that intrude in our lives can become the driver of deeper faith.

---

[10]Jeremiah 29.11.
[11]*The Hiding Place* by Corrie ten Boom, with J. and E. Sherrill (New York: Bantam, 1971).
[12]Hebrews 11.1.
[13]Mark 15.34.
[14]2 Corinthians 4.18.

DECEMBER 21

Christmas . . . and refugees

An angel of the Lord appeared to Joseph in a dream and said,
'Get up. Take the child and his mother and flee to Egypt.'

MATTHEW 2.13

We often hear people speak of the 'spirit of Christmas'. They mean by that phrase the ideal of peace on earth and of kindness towards other people.

There is, sadly, another aspect to the 'spirit of Christmas'. That aspect is the cruel barbarism that characterizes those who forced Mary and Joseph to leave their home and become numbered among the rootless, displaced people of the world. Mary and Joseph were, within the space of a few years, what we today would call refugees, exiles, migrant workers,[1] asylum seekers and homeless.

---

[1] See 19 December, note 1.

The life events and dislocation that Mary and Joseph faced were the result of political events over which they had no control. Joseph and Mary had to travel from Nazareth to Bethlehem to register for a census initiated by Augustus.[2] Herod's insecurity initiated a pogrom of young boys in Bethlehem and the surrounding area. As a result, Mary and Joseph were forced to flee to save Jesus from death. Even after Herod's death, Joseph and Mary were not free to live where they wanted because they feared the murderous intentions of Archelaus.[3]

It must have been a harrowing experience to be pregnant, then to give birth and to nurture a young child in the context of that sort of political and social turmoil. As we have already seen in earlier reflections, Mary would have been separated from family and friends, and from the networks of support that would have helped her in the later stages of pregnancy, the birth itself and the early days of motherhood. She would also have been far from what was familiar, at a time of change and uncertainty. We do not know if she had prepared for being away from home with a young baby. I wonder what Joseph did to earn money to pay for food, accommodation and the things that would be needed for a newborn child.

Children's picture books often portray Jesus as having clean blankets and sleeping in a warm, cosy stable. It was nothing like

---

[2] Luke 2.1–4.
[3] Matthew 1.13–23. Archelaus was Herod's son and succeeded his father on his father's death in 4 BC. He was known as an exceedingly cruel man.

that, and Mary probably had very little with her for a newborn baby. I have often wondered whether anyone took pity on this young mother and offered her practical and emotional support as she gave birth and in the weeks following.

We know that throughout the world, events such as these happen countless times every day, as war and political conflict lead to people having to flee their homes seeking safety. We know, for example, that when the Nazis deported Jewish people during the Second World War, they made no concessions for pregnant or lactating mothers. Recently, there was a report in the press about a young woman in the Middle East who was pregnant on 25 December. She was detained for several hours at a checkpoint. She started to bleed, but the politics of the situation made no concession to her situation. Her baby died for lack of the medical care that the woman was seeking on the other side of the checkpoint at one of the borders in the Holy Land.

I have often wondered about that mother and about the heartlessness of the politics that denied her access to medical help. The baby of that young, Middle Eastern mother died on the day we celebrate the birth of Jesus, born to *another* young Middle Eastern mother centuries before.

Though events such as these are, sadly, common, they cause immeasurable suffering to the people who experience them, and emotional scarring and trauma that often never go away. We would do well to begin to think about the practical difficulties

Mary and Joseph would have gone through. We would also do well to think about the long-term scars their experiences may have left them with.

For those of us who have lived in the United Kingdom all our lives, we do not often think about what it must be like to be 'displaced' and to have refugee status. Yet we are surrounded by people who are (or who were at one time) displaced and refugees. I have worked alongside two survivors of the 'Kinder Transport' of the Second World War. Some of us may have close friends or colleagues who arrived in the United Kingdom at some point during their lives due to political conflict in their home of origin. (Contrary to popular myth, their welcome in the United Kingdom would not always have been kind, generous and loving.) Most days in newspapers and on television, there are reports about people who have been uprooted because of political events or natural disasters. We have no excuse for not knowing about these people, and at least beginning to reflect about their suffering and anguish.

If Joseph with his young family fled to the United Kingdom today, what sort of reception would they receive?

Would they be welcomed and supported? How easy would it be for them to access housing and medical help? Would they find people who were willing to help them unravel the consequences of the trauma they had experienced? Alternatively, would they suffer racist abuse? Would they be denied the means to earn a living and establish social independence?

A little talked about and almost forgotten Christian virtue is to show hospitality and welcome to strangers and outsiders. The Old Testament calls strangers and outsiders 'aliens' and urges us to welcome and include them, not least because the Jewish people were themselves at one time in that condition. In the New Testament, Hebrews 13.2 carries on that tradition. The verse urges us to show hospitality to strangers because some thereby 'entertain angels' without realizing that they have done that.

Even without the encouragement of the Old Testament teaching about 'aliens' and its reaffirmation and restatement in the New Testament in Hebrews 13.2, one would have thought that Christians would excel at welcoming refugees, displaced people, homeless people and political exiles because Jesus and his family experienced each of those conditions.

There is an additional reason why Christians should excel at the virtue of hospitality and welcoming strangers.

In Matthew 25.31–46 Jesus speaks about those who feed the hungry, who give drink to the thirsty and who welcome the stranger. He also speaks of those who clothe the naked and who visit the sick and imprisoned. In other words, Jesus is speaking about those who show compassion for the vulnerable, the despised, the weak and the dispossessed. God reckons such service as also being done to Jesus who himself knew what it was to be vulnerable, despised, weak and dispossessed.

Christmas *is* about a baby, about shepherds and about Magi. It *is* about God's intervention in human affairs and it *is* about the gift of a saviour.

It is *also* about heartbreaking and cruel suffering that ordinary people faced because people with power acted with unprincipled brutality to promote their own self-interested ends.

The same abuses happen today. All too often, we choose to close our hearts and minds to those abuses. We might not see at firsthand the sort of suffering and abuse that Jesus and his family faced. However, if we are alert, we could see rather more than we do and be more engaged than we are. To close our hearts to those who suffer is, Jesus says, to close our hearts to him.

How can we close our hearts to those in our community who stand in need of our compassion, if to serve such people is also to serve Jesus? The sobering fact of Matthew 25 is that the ground of the authenticity of our faith is the way we treat the vulnerable. If we mistreat, neglect or despise them, we bring into question not only our claim to faith but also our hope of salvation.

In addition to reflecting on the significance of the baby born to be king, on the shepherds and on the Magi, we can also admit to the horror of other aspects of the first Christmas. It may help us to practise, in obedience to Jesus' teachings and with the compassion that God gives, the ideal of showing love to the stranger and the dispossessed, and to care for the outcast.

Christmas . . . and loss

A voice was heard in Ramah,
weeping and much lamenting,
Rachel was weeping for her children;
she did not want to be comforted,
because they were dead.

MATTHEW 2.18

The first time I went back to our local church after the birth of our first child was in late December. I still remember clearly that the text for the sermon was Matthew 2.16–18. The sermon was about the massacre Herod instigated against all boys aged 2 and under in the Bethlehem area. As I cradled our newborn daughter, the horror of Herod's brutality became apparent to me, as it had not been before. I could not bear to think about the slaughter that had taken place. In ways I had not been able to imagine before I became a mother, I then began to realize how mothers in Jerusalem at that time might have felt.

Bad things happen at Christmas, as at any other time of the year. Somehow, we do not expect this. When awful things happen at Christmas, some people say it is unjust and unfair. For those filled with emotional pain, Christmas can seem a particularly cruel time. A friend who was grieving for the loss of a close relative who had died shortly before Christmas said to me, 'It feels like there's a party going on around me, and I'm not a part of it.' While most people (in the words of an anonymously authored carol) may 'Rejoice and be merry, in songs and in mirth' at the time of Christmas, there are some who hurt and grieve.

People die at Christmas, as at any other time of year.

When loved ones die during the time around Christmas, this means that future anniversaries will fall during Christmas time. Anniversaries are important. It can be emotionally very difficult to negotiate at Christmas the anniversary of loss through death alongside festive celebrations. It is also hard to prepare for Christmas at the same time as grieving for a loved one who has died.

Christmas is also a time when people get together with their families. The cruel reality for some is that a loved family member will not be present at this time.

I remember what one friend told me. She was out Christmas shopping, and she saw something in a shop. Automatically, she found herself thinking, 'Joe would love that.' But her son, Joe, had died some years earlier, and the reminder that she would not again buy him Christmas presents, or give him a stocking, or cook him a Christmas meal, or watch him open his presents, came with fresh pain.

Another difficulty faced at the time of Christmas is to prepare for the death of a loved one, knowing that this is likely to be the last Christmas the loved one will celebrate with us and we with the loved one. Someone I know, whose parent was dying, bought a video camera as a family Christmas present. He made sure that the present was unwrapped early on Christmas day and used to capture that Christmas on film. Unspoken words communicated that this was almost certainly the last Christmas to be spent with the last surviving parent, in anticipation of what, in that family, would be another untimely death. The pain remained unexpressed, but was present.

We associate Christmas with families and presents, with writing Christmas cards and frenetic shopping, with making mince pies, eating and drinking. Maybe, too, some of us associate Christmas with making some time to think about a baby born 2,000 years ago as the saviour of the world. All too often we forget that, after the first Christmas, innocent children were slaughtered and parents and families faced the harsh realities of cruel bereavement. Grief was very much part of the first Christmas.

Anyone who reads the news regularly will be familiar with pictures and graphic descriptions of children slaughtered during war and strife. The first Christmas was no different; it has been no different at any time before and since. Edmund Sears' carol 'It came upon a Christmas clear' express this clearly in phrases such as 'man, at war with man' and 'the woes of sin and strife'.

The pain of loss and bereavement can be, for some, almost unbearable at Christmas. Those who feel such unbearable pain often do not want to take part in many of the celebrations of the season.

It is not wrong to feel that way. How can one 'Rejoice and be merry in songs and in mirth' while honestly facing the pain of losing a loved one? Rachel (here spoken of representatively as the mother of deceased children) refused to be comforted.[1] The implication is that being consoled is not possible following brutal loss. We are likely to feel the same.

For others, Christmas can be a time when they are filled with guilt and shame about the past, especially as they think about what they cannot now put right. I wonder, for example, about the guilt, grief and trauma that some of Herod's soldiers may have felt as they reflected, in later years, about the young children they had slaughtered in Bethlehem. Some will have 'brushed off' the pangs of conscience. They may have said to themselves that they did what they did as part of their duty

---

[1] Matthew 2.18.

as soldiers. In all likelihood, there will have been others, who later in life suffered guilt and shame, perhaps as they looked at their own children. We all carry guilt and shame about issues that are from our past. How we deal with these issues is important.

Perhaps the issues you face at Christmas are not so much to do with the grief and bereavement that arise from a death or from guilt about the past. Perhaps they have to do with what we all face from time to time when life is hard. We may be facing our own *annus horribilis* (horrible year), as the Queen said she had in 1992.

I think Mary had an *annus horribilis* in the year that Jesus was born, despite the great blessing of becoming a mother. She had faced disgrace during pregnancy and enormous discomfort during the latter days of the pregnancy. Bethlehem was teeming with people, displaced because of the Roman census. Through no fault of her own, she was temporarily homeless. She was probably frightened about giving birth in a strange place, without family support and in bleak conditions. She had to flee to Egypt as a refugee shortly after the birth. No doubt, she would have heard about the slaughter of all male children in Bethlehem under the age of 2. I do not doubt that Mary's joy at having a newborn child (and one that she had been told would be so significant in God's purposes) was muted because of the events happening around her.

So what do we do with suffering, bereavement, hurt and hardship around the time of Christmas? Do we react in the way of someone I knew, who said with some bitterness, 'No-one had better die next year. I want a better Christmas'? (Can we control when people die?) Do we say, as someone I know said, 'My Christmas is ruined'? (Is Christmas ours to be owned?)

For those with faith, there is a place to grieve, since grief is part of the Christmas story. There is also a place to remember that the Christmas story, in its wider context, ends with restoration, healing, forgiveness and life. The pain will go and God will put all things right. Revelation 21.1–4 says there will be a new heaven and a new earth, where there will be no weeping, death, mourning or pain.

Suffering and Christmas *can* go together, and they *did* go together at the first Christmas. More often than we think, they *do* go together.

Even if we do not feel like celebrating at Christmas, we can still give ourselves permission to be thankful for the birth of Jesus. This does not mean that we need necessarily to enjoy all the trappings that now go with Christmas. It simply means that we can taste something of the real meaning of the first Christmas.

If you grieve and hurt at Christmas, so perhaps did Mary. She too carried a heavy burden. We may mourn, yet still be thankful for the birth of Jesus and for what that means.

Christmas . . . and food

*The Son of Man came eating and drinking, and they say,
'Look, a glutton and a drunkard'.*

MATTHEW 11.19

I read a press report in November 2008 about a man who, since 1994, had celebrated Christmas each day of the year with a full roast dinner, a bottle of champagne, a Christmas card and a present!

Christmas *is* a time to celebrate (though I think celebrating every day is a bit excessive), and that is why most of us buy one another presents, exchange cards and have a special meal together. Jesus commended celebrations, and that meant eating as well as other things, when there was something to celebrate.[1]

For most of us, there is a lot of eating at Christmas, and many of us look forward to some of our favourite food at Christmas.

---

[1] Mark 2.19 and Matthew 11.19.

In 2008, we threw away tradition (and caution) and asked our three children what they would like to eat for Christmas lunch.

One said, 'Roasted parsnips, Pringles and sausages wrapped in bacon'. Another said, 'Pizza and Pringles'. The other asked for tuna sandwiches in white bread, cut into triangles with no crusts . . . and Pringles. This is what we gave our children to eat that Christmas day. They were delighted.

Many of us enjoy Christmas and the special food we traditionally have. The downside is that many of us eat too much at Christmas and start the New Year with a resolution to join a gym and lose weight. (By February or March most have stopped going to the gym!)

For people who are overweight and who are trying to reduce their weight, Christmas can be an immensely difficult time. There are temptations and pressures all around. I know of one mother who in mid-December ate the chocolate she had bought for her children's stockings. She had to hide the wrappers and go out and buy more, concealing her guilt and harbouring self-disgust.

Around the time of Christmas, people often eat many of the things that a reducing diet prohibits. It is hard not to, as the traditions of the season often mean we buy or cook food we do not eat every day. At work and social gatherings, rich food is often freely available. If an overweight person declines to eat some of these festive foods, well-meaning people sometimes put them under pressure to change their mind. They might be labelled a 'killjoy' or be told 'just one won't hurt; you can diet after Christmas'. If they stick to their diet, they might feel resentful that other people can enjoy food but they have to deny themselves. Others may eat to excess the foods that at other times they would avoid. Those who eat rich festive food are likely to be consumed by guilt afterwards and might berate themselves for having 'no will power'. The food is there, people want them to eat it and a part of them wants to eat it . . . and they find themselves in a 'no win' situation.

Christmas can also be a very difficult time for those who have serious psychological issues to do with food and weight. I work with people who suffer from eating disorders (anorexia nervosa, bulimia nervosa and binge eating disorder) and I see at firsthand how miserable Christmas can be for such people and for their families.

Most people do not understand what is going on in the mind of someone with an eating disorder. For someone with an eating disorder, Christmas can be a threatening and miserable time, because issues to do with food eclipse any idea of celebration or worship at Christmas. People suffering from eating disorders usually become consumed by planning what they are and are not going to allow themselves to eat because they are frightened at the thought of gaining weight. So they become embroiled in battles within themselves regarding what is permitted and what is prohibited in the way of food consumption. They often fear they will be regarded as 'greedy', of being 'overindulgent', or of having 'more than other people'.

Because eating (and, in particular, eating appreciatively and eating a lot) are so much part of the festive season and of socializing, those with eating disorders can find it very difficult to mix with family over a festive meal at Christmas. When some choose to eat alone or not to eat much, other members of the family may be hurt or resentful. Conflict commonly arises. One person I knew chose to prepare for herself a bowl of cornflakes on Christmas day and to eat these alone. This was so she would avoid having to eat a traditional Christmas meal with her family. Conflict followed.

This sad picture seems to apply equally for those with faith and for those without.

Having an eating disorder is not about lack of faith or about failing to understand that God loves us as we are. In my view, it is not a spiritual issue at all. It is a psychological disorder to do with terror embedded in eating and the morbid fear of gaining weight. It is not that such people are at fault, or do not want to celebrate Christmas. It is that they feel unable to celebrate Christmas in the way that is traditional for our culture, with food. Christian charity means that we should respect their preference, and find other ways of celebrating that they can enter into.

It is good to remember where our true value lies. God loves us for who we are, not for the size or shape or weight that we are. Jesus did not tell us that we may celebrate only if we are a certain size and shape, and only if we eat or do not eat certain things.

The issue of celebrating with food does not just affect people who are on reducing diets or who have eating disorders. It also affects other people, people perhaps like you or me. For such people, spending too much money and time on food and eating too much might induce uncomfortable feelings of guilt. We have so much and we spend so much, yet two-thirds of the world's population is undernourished, and one of those thirds is starving. It can feel markedly dissonant to celebrate with lavish food and, at the same time, to remember the world's poor.

It seems to me that there is a place to celebrate; that means (among other things) to eat, drink and be merry. It is good to mark out the season as special by eating and drinking special things. Yet, Jesus would have us remember the poor. I suspect this means to eat and drink with more moderation than our culture encourages. I suspect it also may perhaps mean that we should regard the season as one for sharing some of the riches that we in the developed world enjoy with those who have significantly less.

One small step that we have made as a family is to give gifts, when we can, through agencies such as Oxfam or World Vision, or similar organizations, to Third World causes. We give these gifts in place of gifts to some family members (but not our children!) and to friends. Others we know do the same.

To give or 'receive' school dinners, vaccinations, fruit trees, goats, equipment to purify water, school books, mosquito nets, and so on are part of what it means 'to bring good news to the poor . . . and to proclaim the year of the Lord's favour'.[2] It is, I suspect, to share in the work Jesus did when he came to earth as a human being.

I am *not* urging that we should stop celebrating, nor am I urging that we should stop giving Christmas presents to one another. I *am* urging that we should celebrate with our eyes and hearts on others who have rather less than we do, and that we give to those in need as part of our celebration.

---

[2]Luke 4.18–19.

Christmas . . . and Jesus the man

The Word was God . . . and became fully human

JOHN 1.1, 14

I suspect that many of us think that Jesus was exempt from much of the day-to-day grind of life that we face. The fact that he was God in human form somehow protected him, so we might think, from experiencing life as it really is.

Some of the carols we sing seem to reinforce the view that Jesus was not quite properly a human being. In 'Hark! The herald angels sing' by Charles Wesley, we sing about the Godhead 'veiled in flesh'. This implies that Jesus' bodily form was a mere cover. It was like an item of clothing that can be taken on and off at will, and not constitutive of Jesus being embodied (like you and me) as a human being. Thomas Pestel's carol 'Behold the great creator makes' has the same idea: it refers to Jesus having 'a robe of flesh'. 'Of the Father's heart begotten' (originally written in Latin) perhaps fudges the issue by saying that Jesus 'assumed' (what does this word really mean?) a human body that was 'frail and feeble, doomed to die'.

If we take what these carols seem to imply, we may infer (in my view, mistakenly) that Jesus' bodily form is no more than an external guise that he temporarily took on. We may also infer (I think also mistakenly) that Jesus was never truly who he seemed to be. He would have been like an actor, who plays a part in a film or play, skilful at convincing an audience but different from the person portrayed.

The Gospels are clear that Jesus was fully a human being. He knew what life was like, and he experienced it, just as we 'ordinary' people do, with no special privileges, get-outs or exemptions.[1]

For example, Jesus became tired from work. At times, he craved to be on his own, away from people. He wept and grieved when friends died. He prayed, he slept, he partied and, although we often lose sight of this, he could be very funny when he spoke. (The parables made people smile. What of the foolish farmer who scattered seed here, there and everywhere? What of the dishonest manager who ludicrously

---

[1]See also the reflection headed 15 December.

defrauded his boss to save his own skin? What of the woman who calls in her neighbours to say she had found a lost coin?)

As with other human beings, Jesus knew what it was to be deeply afraid and troubled about death and suffering. We see this in the accounts of Jesus' inner conflicts when he was at Gethsemane, for example.[2] He was also tempted to sin and not exempt from the struggles that temptation brings.[3] However, and here is an important difference from you and me, the writers of the New Testament say that, despite the temptations, Jesus did not sin.

So, if Jesus did not sin, is he like us or not? Is he as much a human being as you or I? Or is he something slightly different?

Of course, the fact that Jesus did not sin does makes him *in that respect* different from us. We all sin; he did not. In consequence, he was not marred with the guilt, shame and scarring that we have because we sin.

That is where the difference ends. The difference, such as it is, is a difference of *quality* (though he was human, he did not sin), not *category* (he was not human and so did not sin). The Athanasian Creed expresses this clearly. It helps us understand that, in the context of the traditions of the church, Jesus *is* flesh and blood and as human as we are, even though he is without sin.

---

[2]Matthew 26.36–46, Mark 14.32–42 and Luke 22.40–46.
[3]See, for example, Matthew 4.1–11 and Hebrews 5.7–9.

The implications of insisting that Jesus is fully human but did not sin are hard to work out, and even paradoxical. However, in the wider context of Christian theology, the point is important, especially when it comes to how the New Testament writers say that God draws people into the life of faith.

One way of understanding the way God draws us into the life of faith is to say that, as Jesus is fully one of us and one with us, so we can become fully like him. To paraphrase the words of Irenaeus (c. AD 130–200) that are often quoted in this context, Jesus became what we are (human beings) so that by being united in him we might become who he is. Jesus entered fully into being human and now, by faith in him, we can enter fully into his resurrection life. There can be, as Morna Hooker has expressed it, an 'interchange'.[4]

We do this if, as John says, we 'receive' Jesus.[5] Receiving Jesus is part of the process of 'interchange', for as we receive Jesus, Jesus thereby receives us.

Let me explain what I mean by 'receive Jesus' with an example. (The example does not fully take into account every element of 'interchange' in the process of salvation. It highlights only what it means to enter into the life of Christ.)

---

[4]On this, see especially her *Not Ashamed of the Gospel: New Testament Interpretations of the Death of Christ* (Carlisle: Paternoster Press, 2004).
[5]John 1.12.

You may have sent me a Christmas gift by post. If I refuse to accept delivery of the gift you sent, it will not enter my home but will remain in the possession of the carrier who tried to deliver it. I do not therefore receive it. Alternatively, I may accept delivery of the gift, gratefully receiving it because I know it has come from you. However, there is more I must do if the gift is truly to become mine: I must also unwrap it, accept it into my possession and both use and enjoy it.

In the same way, we may choose to reject the gift of Jesus that God offers or we may accept God's gift, welcoming Jesus and opening up our lives to him.[6]

Some people remember a clear point when they became Christians by 'receiving' Christ. I am one such person. Before the point when I 'received' Christ, I knew I was not a Christian and I knew I did not want to be a Christian. There came a time when I realized that to continue to resist what I knew to be true was both futile and personally dishonest, and so I welcomed, albeit diffidently and reluctantly, the Jesus who I knew wanted to be received.

For others, in contrast, there is no such clear-cut point of conversion. Faith is something these people have grown into, often from childhood. Their story has mainly to do with maturing and growing into a deeper appreciation of what they have believed for as long as they can remember.

---

[6]This borrows the language of Revelation 3.20 in a different context.

Whichever type of person you are, what is important is that you know you are *continuing* to receive Jesus. (At this point also, the analogy of the parcel I gave above breaks down, for entering into Jesus' experience of death, burial and resurrection is not a case of 'receiving' Jesus only once.) The New Testament writers link becoming a Christian (once at a point in time) with being a Christian (a continuing experience), and say that both are necessary if either is to have continuing validity. Being a Christian is about going on receiving Jesus, on a day-by-day basis, continually yielding to him and welcoming him afresh.

Many people find that to receive the bread and the wine in a communion service is a helpful way to express the longing to go on receiving Jesus. The bread and the wine represent Jesus. Physically to receive the bread and wine into our bodies can be a powerful expression of our longing to go on receiving Jesus and his nurturing life. Just as we need to eat every day for ongoing nourishment and sustenance, so we need to go on receiving the ongoing spiritual nourishment and sustenance that Jesus gives if we are to live out the sort of life he wants us to live.

As we receive Jesus and go on receiving him (in whichever ways best express our faith), so Jesus makes us one with him. His death on the cross becomes our death on the cross; his burial becomes our burial; and his rising to new life becomes our rising to new life. True, we will all die physically, as Jesus did. For Christians, however, physical death is not the end. It is the gateway to something incomparably more splendid, a new form of reality and existence. We become confident about that new reality and existence as we go on receiving Jesus.

As I hope you can see, the Christmas story of Jesus being one of us is at the heart of the Christian faith and not a sentimental 'bolt on'. Liturgically, it offers us an annual reminder to go on receiving Jesus afresh, and to welcome him into our lives. We can all, Christian and seeker alike, sing the last verse of Phillips Brooks' carol 'O Little Town of Bethlehem' on *any* day of the year and especially on Christmas day, praying that Jesus would 'be born in us' and continue to 'abide with us'.

Christmas

Jesus Christ is the same yesterday, today and for ever.

HEBREWS 13.8

One of my earliest memories is of a Christmas tree in our home.

It was so tall that my father had to cut off the top of the tree. I remember its coloured lights, with big, old-fashioned bulbs. I also remember the smell of the pine needles, and my mother saying that she could not clean the needles from the carpet when they dropped from the tree.

I also remember as a child being very, very excited on Christmas Eve and waking early on Christmas Day to see what was at the end of my bed.

I recall wonderful Christmas lunches at my grandmother's flat. (We called this grandmother 'Grandma Puff' because she was a chain smoker!) There was always a Christmas pudding with threepenny (pronounced 'thrupenny') pieces[1] and silver sixpences[2] concealed in it.

My parents used to go out to a party on Christmas evening. That night, my sister and I would sleep in my grandmother's lounge, with the Christmas tree lights left on all night, in camp beds and each of us with a hot-water bottle. We slept under feather eiderdowns, in bed linen that I thought smelt of pastry. (I now know this to be the smell of starch.)

Excitement, wonder and fun were the hallmarks of those early Christmas Days.

As the years have gone by, I have lost the *childhood* excitement, wonder and fun of Christmas. Threepenny pieces and silver sixpences have long since gone. We would not dare to put them in Christmas puddings now, as they would be regarded as a choking hazard. Sadly, 'Grandma Puff' died many years ago. In our home we now have a modest, artificial Christmas tree. My back aches when I sleep on a camp bed and I do not like hot-water bottles any more!

Christmas *remains* a time of excitement and wonder for me, but for altogether different reasons. I have grown up (some would say that I am now old!) and I value different things.

---

[1]A 12-sided brass coin, about 21 mm in diameter and worth three (pre-decimalization) pence (£0.005).
[2]These coins were minted until 1947 and were part silver. After 1946, they were cupronickel. They were worth six (pre-decimalization) pence (£0.025).

Having become a Christian during my adulthood, I now look on Christmas in a new way.

These days, I rejoice about what I regard as timeless. I rejoice that Jesus has now come and points us to God. I marvel at God's gifts of love and goodness that we see at Christmas. I marvel that God reconciles us to himself through what began at the first Christmas. I celebrate that God has poured his grace and mercy into us in a new way because Jesus has been born. I delight that God continues to pour that grace and mercy into us as we believe in him.

Of course, since we now have three children who get excited about Christmas, Melanie and I enter into their sense of fun and pleasure at Christmas. We take delight in what Christmas means to them, and their joy means a lot to us. Our principal focus, though, is different from what we valued when we ourselves were children.

Whenever you may be reading this (whether or not it is on Christmas day), we trust that you will celebrate what Christmas means with renewed excitement and wonder, and with deepened understanding. If you *are* reading this on Christmas day, we also wish you a very happy Christmas.

'They think it's all over . . .'

We have a great cloud of witnesses surrounding us. We should lay aside every impediment and every sinful distraction . . . fixing our eyes on Jesus.

HEBREWS 12.1–2

If you are reading this on Boxing Day, it will almost certainly be true that on Christmas Eve, after the shops closed at the end of the day's trading, some shop staff will have been asked to remain behind.

Why?

It will have been to take down the Christmas decorations and to prepare the shops for reopening either on 26 December or on 27 December for 'The Sales'.

All the Christmas spending, all the preparation, all the advertising . . . for an event that will last for only one day, Christmas day.

All the excitement, all the parties and all the stress . . . for an event that will have been erased from the public face of the shops the night before the event began.

No wonder so many people have an awful sense of let down at the end of Christmas day. 'Yes, it was a lovely meal', they may think as the day draws to a close, 'and yes, the children did like their presents. But already one of the presents is broken and the children are so out of routine from the excitement that it will take until the end of the school holidays to get them to calm down.'

You might wonder of Christmas in the twenty-first century, 'Is it all worth it?'

If I am truthful, I do not think it is worth it, for just one day of festivity and celebration. If this is all there is to Christmas, with weeks of preparation and one day of celebration, I would be deeply frustrated. One day in the year cannot satisfy us in the way we long that it should. It cannot do justice to what Christians are truly seeking to celebrate.

But Christmas is not about one day in the year!

If we think Christmas means '25 December', I fear we have allowed the secularization of the festival to shape the way we celebrate and think about Christmas.

There is not one day to Christmas, but at least 12 days to Christmas. Though we sing 'The Twelve Days of Christmas', we may not have thought about the meaning and context of the song.

Traditionally, 'Christmastide' lasted from the night of Christmas day until the night of the eve of the Epiphany on

5 January, 12 days in total. It was a period of feasting and merry-making, and as 'The Twelve Days of Christmas' suggests, some even gave gifts on each of the 12 days of Christmas. In some Church traditions, 'Christmastide' lasts from 25 December until 2 February, for a total of 40 days.[1]

In case you shudder as you read this, I am not suggesting 12 or 40 days of parties and presents!

What I am suggesting is that we should not sigh with relief at the end of Christmas day and think, 'That's Christmas over for another year.' It is not like Kenneth Wolstenholme's famous commentary during the 1966 football World Cup, when he began to say (in the dying seconds of the final match), 'They think it's all over . . . it is now.'

Most definitely, after Christmas day it is not 'all over'.

If we have truly entered into what Christmas is about, we will want to celebrate what God has done at the first Christmas well beyond 25 December. We will long to go on rejoicing that God has fully entered the human condition so that we might share in who he is. We will want to praise God because, since God came among us in the way he did with Jesus, we can now know who God is, what he is like and what he asks of us.

---

[1] In the Anglican tradition, 2 February is called 'Presentation of Christ in the Temple' (see Luke 2.22–38 and the reflections headed 17 and 18 December) or 'Candlemas'. In Durham Cathedral where we worship, the Cathedral's Christmas tree is pointedly left in place until *after* 2 February.

These truths are not truths to celebrate on only one day a year. In fact, I do not think it is possible adequately to celebrate these truths on only one day a year. What we need is a sustained period of celebration, so that the truths take root in our worship and understanding.

Advent helps us to be ready to celebrate, and to celebrate wisely, thoughtfully and 'in Spirit and in truth' on Christmas day and on every other day.[2]

After Christmas Day and in the weeks that follow, we should continue to make the wonder of Christmas the particular focus of our worship. It is not possible to move on after Christmas Day, if we say to ourselves, 'That's Christmas and all that it means celebrated. We will do it again in 12 months time. It's over and done with for another year. Now we think about something else.'

It is *absurd* to think that we can adequately express our worship and celebration of what God has done through the birth of Jesus in just one day. How can we do justice to the magnitude of what God has done if *on Christmas day only* that is our special focus? It is like trying to eat a five-course *cordon bleu* meal served with fine wines in fewer than 5 minutes.

Most of us will want (and need) a sustained period to express our gratitude and wonder that 'the Word became flesh and dwelt among us'.[3] It will take until the end of the Christmas

---

[2] John 4.24.
[3] John 1.14.

season (whether that is 12 or 40 days or some other number of days) for us to do this. Our continuing gratitude should infuse our worship in the months after that. If that gratitude begins to wane, as it most likely will in the course of time, then the following Advent will prepare us for Christmas again and rekindle our zeal and worship. We take part in an annual cycle of celebration that renews our focus on the birth of Jesus and what that means, so that it becomes part of the bedrock of our faith and worship.

On 10 November 1942 in the middle of the Second World War, Prime Minister Winston Churchill made a speech at the Lord Mayor's lunch at the Mansion House in London. The speech followed a military victory at El Alamein in North Africa.

In closing, I quote his words and invite you today to think of them as referring not to a military victory but to Christmas Day: Christmas Day, I suggest, 'is not the end. It is not even the beginning of the end. But it is, perhaps, the end of the beginning.'

We wish you great joy as we celebrate, on any day and at any time of the year, 'our God contracted to a span, incomprehensibly made man'.[4] We say, with Paul, 'thanks be to God for his gift that is wonderful beyond words'.[5]

---

[4]Charles Wesley in his carol, 'Let earth and heaven combine'.
[5]2 Corinthians 9.15.

INDEX